WHY SO MANY CHRISTIANS HAVE LEFT THE FAITH

MICHAEL L. BROWN, PhD

CHARISMA
HOUSE

Most Charisma Media products are available at special quantity discounts for bulk purchase for sales promotions, premiums, fundraising, and educational needs. For details, call us at (407) 333-0600 or visit our website at www.charismamedia.com.

WHY SO MANY CHRISTIANS HAVE LEFT THE FAITH by Michael L. Brown, PhD
Published by Charisma House, an imprint of Charisma Media
600 Rinehart Road, Lake Mary, Florida 32746

Cataloging-in-Publication Data is on file with the Library of Congress.
International Standard Book Number: 978-1-63641-169-9
E-book ISBN: 978-1-63641-170-5

23 24 25 26 27 — 987654321
Printed in the United States of America

CONTENTS

PREFACE

SINCE YOU ARE reading this book right now, my guess is that you're reading for one of two reasons. Either you are a Christian who is concerned about other believers leaving the faith (perhaps someone close to you), or you yourself have left the faith (or have many questions about your faith). Am I right? If so, you are reading the right book. (If you're reading it for other reasons, I hope you'll find it helpful as well!)

What you'll find in the pages that follow is anything but a stale, theological analysis or a judgmental, finger-wagging tome. Wherever you find yourself—in the faith, outside the faith, or wavering—you will not be scolded or lectured. Instead, I will explore why so many believers have deconstructed, especially here in America, offering practical responses to each and every reason.

Personally, as a Jewish believer in Jesus since late 1971 who has been challenged in my faith every step of the way since then, I think it's important to ask serious questions and seek serious answers. In fact, I not only welcome such questions.

I solicit them. Truth is our friend, not our enemy. As for the Bible, as you'll see in the pages that follow, there are many good reasons it has stood the test of time and the test of criticism, remaining the world's best-selling book to this day.

I'm aware, of course, that some Christians do not believe anyone can truly fall away from the faith, citing 1 John 2:19 in support of their views. There John writes, "They went out from us, but they did not really belong to us. For if they had belonged to us, they would have remained with us; but their going showed that none of them belonged to us."

This remains true to this day. Many people appear to be "with us" for a season, only to show their true colors by leaving. John refers to such people in this verse. But that is not to say that every single person who leaves the church is a false convert. Certainly not. To the contrary, it is all too easy to write off those who have departed from the faith by saying, "They never really believed."

Again, it is true that some were false converts. But many were true converts, and I take their stories seriously. Why did they renounce their faith? Was it intellectual? Was it experiential? Was it a combination of both? Did they fall morally before they changed their theology? Did church hypocrisy drive them away? Did bad theology distort their expectations?

These are the questions we put on the table in this book (among many others), and in each and every case I do my best to offer solid, thoughtful, intellectually sound, morally defensible, theologically rigorous, and fully compassionate answers. I hope and pray that you will find them helpful, informative, and perhaps even life changing and faith building. For some, perhaps the answers will even be faith saving or faith restoring. May it be so!

What I can tell you with certainty, speaking for myself, is this: God is absolutely faithful, and His Word is absolutely trustworthy—and I say that having experienced the tragedies and pains of life, like everyone else who has lived long enough, and having been challenged for decades by brilliant rabbis and professors and activists and nonbelievers of every stripe.

But that is my story, and you have your own. My prayer is that God would use this book to bring you to a deeper place of certainty in your faith, secure in the Lord, enjoying Him with both heart and mind, thriving rather than living in denial and pain.

As always, I express my appreciation to Stephen Strang, Debbie Marrie, Adrienne Gaines, and the expert editing, fact-checking, marketing, and graphics team at Charisma Media. And I remain indebted to my bride since 1976, Nancy, herself a former staunch atheist, who is more committed to following the truth at any cost than any person I know.

> For we cannot do anything against the truth, but only for the truth.
> —2 CORINTHIANS 13:8

CHAPTER 1

THERE REALLY IS A PROBLEM

THE NEWS WAS jarring and disturbing, captured in this July 29, 2019, headline in *USA Today*: "He wrote the Christian case against dating. Now he's splitting from his wife and faith." Yes, Joshua Harris, the man who wrote the best-selling 1997 book *I Kissed Dating Goodbye*, the man who played a key role in what became known as "purity culture," the man who pastored an influential megachurch in Maryland, this respected Christian leader was now leaving his wife after some twenty years of marriage and was no longer following Jesus. *Joshua Harris?*

Harris noted in an Instagram post that he had "undergone a massive shift in regard to [his] faith in Jesus."[1] He stated that he had repented "of my self-righteousness, my fear-based approach to life, the teaching of my books, my views of women in the church, and my approach to parenting to name a few."

He continued that he "specifically" wanted to apologize to the LGBTQ+ community, saying that he was "sorry" for views on sexuality he had espoused in his books and at the pulpit. "I regret standing against marriage equality, for not affirming you and your place in the church, and for any ways that my writing and speaking contributed to a culture of exclusion and bigotry. I hope you can forgive me."[2]

Yet it was this same man who, at the age of twenty-one, authored his influential best seller, a book that discouraged young Christian people from dating, a book that emphasized the importance of remaining sexually pure until marriage and encouraged serious courtship leading to marriage. Now he was saying goodbye to it all.

But Harris is not the only Christian leader to renounce his faith in recent years. To the contrary, this is becoming increasingly common, to the point that there is an active call for Christians in general to follow suit and "deconvert," often the final step in the process of "deconstruction." Put another way, Christians are being told, "It's time to question everything you learned, time to read the Bible through new eyes, time to put away your presuppositions and cherished beliefs, and time to be brutally honest with yourself. When you do, you will no longer profess your Christian faith—at least, not in the way you once did. It's time to be enlightened!"

A WORSHIP LEADER LOSES HIS FAITH

There had been no public hint of struggle until August 2019, when Marty Sampson, a popular Hillsong worship leader and songwriter, used his Instagram platform to announce that he was questioning his faith. This prompted me to write an article reaching out to him, saying, "My prayer is that Marty Sampson would have the integrity of heart to seek the truth earnestly, with humility and passion, and that all others with questions will put those questions on the table."[3]

On August 13, the *Christian Post* reported that Sampson had responded to my column, clarifying that he hadn't lost his faith, but it's "on incredibly shaky ground."[4] Sadly, just a little over a week later, he wrote, "It was amazing being one of you, but I'm not any more."[5]

"Time for some real talk," he explained on Instagram (before deleting the post). "I'm genuinely losing my faith..[sic] and it doesn't bother me... like, what bothers me now is nothing... I am so happy now, so at peace with the world.. [sic] it's crazy."

And what, in particular, caused this change of heart and mind? He continued:

> How many preachers fall? Many. No one talks about it. How many miracles happen. Not many. No one talks about it. Why is the Bible full of contradictions? No one talks about it. How can God be love yet send 4 billion people to a place, all coz they don't believe? No one talks about it.

In short, he's "not in" anymore and he desires "genuine truth." But, he claimed, "Science keeps piercing the truth of every religion. Lots of things help people change their lives, not just one version of God." He went on to say that he was "keeping it real" and that people could unfollow him if they wanted to, adding, "I've never been about living my life for others."[6]

Of course, it is easy to respond to Sampson's concerns, as I did in my August 2019 article, reaching out to him rather than condemning him.[7] But that doesn't diminish his own very real loss of faith, nor does it detract from the reality of his own experience, which reflects the experience of many other former Christians. In fact, the number of professing Christians within America has dropped dramatically in the last decade, from 75 percent to 63 percent, while the number of Americans who have no religious affiliation is now up to nearly 30 percent, according to a Pew Research Center report.[8] This is an unprecedented shift since the enacting of national polling. It looks like Marty Sampson, an Australian, has plenty of company worldwide.

A CHRISTIAN ROCK SINGER IS NOW AN AGNOSTIC

Jon Steingard was raised in the church and eventually became the lead singer for the popular Christian rock band Hawk Nelson. Then, in what seemed sudden and quite out of the blue to many of his followers, he too posted on Instagram that he no longer believed what he was singing. His departure from the faith became headline news. On May 27, 2020, CNN announced, "Jonathan Steingard, Christian singer, reveals he no longer believes in God."[9] As he expressed with candor and vulnerability, "I've been terrified to post this for a while—but it feels like it's time for me to be honest. I hope this is not the end of the conversation, but the beginning."

He continued, "After growing up in a Christian home, being a pastor's kid, playing and singing in a Christian band, and having the word 'Christian' in front of most of the things in my life—I am now finding that I no longer believe in God. The last few words of that sentence were hard to write. I still find myself wanting to soften that statement by wording it differently or less specifically—but it wouldn't be as true."[10]

He explained that "the process of getting to that sentence has been several years in the making." However, the public announcement was sudden and shocking, just like the announcements of Joshua Harris and Marty Sampson. Why is this happening so much?

Jon and I engaged in a friendly dialogue about these issues in a mini-debate format made for Christian TV. He was cordial and gracious in expressing his views. He said that he wished he could find a way to hold on to the good things he found in the Bible and the Christian faith without having to believe in the God of the Bible or Christianity.[11] For now, he was identifying as an agnostic while continuing on his journey and search.

How many others are there, just like him, struggling on the inside, wrestling with doubts and questions, but without any of their friends or colleagues or family members or parishioners aware? How many more will soon go public with their own deconversion story?

A FORMER BIBLE SCHOOL PROFESSOR IS NO LONGER A CHRISTIAN

Paul Maxwell earned a PhD from Trinity Evangelical Divinity School, one of the nation's finest and most intellectually rigorous evangelical institutions, and he taught philosophy at Moody Bible Institute, one of the country's most conservative Bible schools. He also contributed to the very popular Desiring God website, which follows in the tradition of the beloved pastor and teacher John Piper. But suddenly, in April 2021, also on Instagram—probably the communication mode of choice for these deconversion announcements because of the platform's popularity with the poster's fan base—he announced that he had abandoned the faith.

He wrote, "I love you guys, and I love all the support and friendships I've built here [Instagram]...I think it's important to say that I'm just not a Christian anymore, and it feels really good. I'm really happy...I'm really happy."

He continued, "I can't wait to discover what kind of connection I can have with all of you beautiful people as I try to figure out what's next....I'm so full of joy for the first time. I love my life for the first time...and I love myself for the first time."[12]

Of course, obedience rather than personal happiness should be the ultimate goal of a follower of Jesus. But how is it that only now, having shed his faith, Dr. Maxwell is finally happy and full of joy—allegedly for the first time? My personal experience of the overwhelming, astounding, mindboggling, inexpressibly glorious joy of the Lord on December 17, 1971, after weeks of deep conviction of sin, revealed the love of God to me through Jesus. In a moment of time, I surrendered my life to Him, pledging never to put a needle in my arm again. I was instantly set free! Prior to that, I was nicknamed Drug Bear and Iron Man because of my intense drug use.

I have experienced that "inexpressible and glorious joy" (1 Pet. 1:8) countless times over the decades, sometimes being so full of God's love, goodness, grace, and favor that I almost want to leap out of my skin. Truly, in His presence is fullness of joy! (See Psalm 16:11.) And how can I describe the sense of deep fulfillment that comes from knowing the Lord personally and having a deep sense of destiny, calling, and purpose? I couldn't imagine living without that.

Yet Paul Maxwell claimed that it was only after he no longer believed that he could say he was "really happy," "so full of joy," and, for the first time, loving his own life. How do we explain that? To ask again, how many others are just like him, studying in our seminaries, teaching in our ministry schools, writing on our blogs, serving as leaders in the body, but themselves joyless and discontent? I do not write this to judge or criticize Maxwell but only to ask an obvious question.

A CHRISTIAN HIP-HOP ARTIST AND APOLOGIST HAS RENOUNCED THE FAITH

Although I was very familiar with the name Joshua Harris prior to his deconversion, I had not heard of Marty Sampson (although I probably knew some of his music) or Jon Steingard or Paul Maxwell. Nor had I heard of Brady Goodwin, better known as Phanatik. But once I learned about his renunciation of the faith (posted via video announcement on Facebook), I found out that he was a greatly loved hip-hop artist and defender of the faith, known for his work in apologetics and music.

Goodwin is not only a founding member of the Grammy-nominated Christian hip-hop group The Cross Movement, he is also a graduate of Westminster Theological Seminary, earning a master's degree there. (Westminster is also a fine theological seminary, known for its conservative biblical stands.) And when he and I talked by Zoom in response to the article I wrote about his departure from the faith, it was clear that he had a serious background in the Bible and theology.[13]

Yet in his January 2022 video announcement, in which he seemed to struggle to get to his point, recognizing how it would sound to many people he loved, he said, "I sent a letter to my church withdrawing my membership and saying [he stumbled in his speech here as he tried to get the words out] that I am denouncing the Christian faith that I have believed, professed, proclaimed, and defended for the last thirty years of my life."[14]

Ironically, Goodwin has stated that his doubts began when he was studying at Lancaster Bible College, only to deepen when he attended Westminster. As summed up by Josh Shepherd:

> Specifically, he said learning how scholars use preexisting "theological commitments" to arrive at translation and interpretation of the biblical text raised questions for him. He compared Christian theology to a Rubik's cube. "I began to look at the faith and say, 'Man you could turn this Rubik's cube any particular way and end up with a different understanding.' And who can say that understanding is right or that understanding is wrong?"[15]

So now we can add Goodwin to the unprecedented number of people who are turning away from Christianity. It's a trend, as shown in that Pew Research report posted December 2021 and mentioned a few pages ago, that seems to be gaining speed.[16] "Self-identified Christians make up 63% of U.S. population in 2021, down from 75% a decade ago." This is an extraordinary, unprecedented decline (at least since polling has been done).

According to that report, "The secularizing shifts evident in American society so far in the 21st century show no signs of slowing. The latest Pew Research Center survey of the religious composition of the United States finds the religiously unaffiliated share of the public is 6 percentage points higher than it was five years ago and 10 points higher than a decade ago.

"Christians continue to make up a majority of the U.S. populace, but their share of the adult population is 12 points lower in 2021 than it was in 2011. In addition, the share of U.S. adults who say they pray on a daily basis has been trending downward, as has the share who say religion is 'very important' in their lives."[17]

As to why so many now fall in the category of "nones" (having no religious affiliation), in a 2018 survey, Pew Research found that "out of several options included in the survey, the most common reason they give is that they question a lot of religious teachings."[18] This is exactly what happened to Goodwin.

But on a personal level, while I deeply sympathize with those who could not find answers to their questions, I experienced the precise opposite of this. That's because from the very beginning my faith was challenged by those who did not share my beliefs, starting with the local rabbi in early 1972 and continuing through my college and grad school years, right up through me earning my PhD. Never once in all that time did I take a single academic class with a professor who shared my faith. Yet the more my faith was challenged and the more I searched for honest answers, the stronger my faith became.

What, then, is the difference between people like Brady Goodwin, who lost his faith while studying with believers, and people like me, whose faith became stronger when studying with unbelievers? How many others within the church share Goodwin's perspective, having more questions than answers? Since his apostasy announcement, he has gone back to the seminary libraries, but *not* to recover his faith. Instead, it is to complete his research *against* the Bible—at least, the Bible as we have read it and received it.

ARE THERE SOLID ANSWERS?

In my public response to "Phanatik" (which opened the door for our dialogue), I asked, "But what about the points he makes in his video? What about the feeling that we can basically make the Bible say whatever we want it to say? Or that it's our prior theological commitments that determine how we understand Scripture?

"Put another way, is there no objective truth when it comes to God and the Bible? Does it come down to, 'You have your truth and I have my truth, but there is no absolute truth'?"

I answered by writing this:

> Speaking candidly, I know all too well what it is to struggle with the faith.
>
> That's because as a Jewish believer in Jesus, from my first moments in the faith, I was challenged over my beliefs. As my dad said to me shortly after my life was transformed in late 1971, "Michael, I'm glad you're off drugs. But we're Jews. We don't believe this."
>
> That led to immediate, intensive interaction with learned rabbis (which has continued for 50 years) along with serious academic study, culminating with a Ph.D. in Near Eastern Languages and Literatures from New York University.[19]

As I just noted, "In all my college and graduate studies, not one of my professors was a Bible-believing Christian. Some were even hostile to the faith, taking every opportunity to ridicule conservative Bible beliefs."

"But," I continued, "the whole reason I earned the degrees that I did (all of which were in ancient languages) was so that I could read the original biblical text in its original cultural and linguistic context, not having to rely on other dictionaries or commentaries to understand what I was reading (although, to be sure, there can be great value in many of those dictionaries, commentaries, and other books)."

And so it was that:

> Over the years, the more I studied and the more I wrestled with objections to my faith, the stronger my faith became. My mind was now in complete harmony with my heart, my intellect now matching my experience.
>
> Others, sadly, have had different experiences and have ended up leaving the faith rather than growing in the faith. And Goodwin is careful to say, "Hey, don't blame seminaries or put this on intellectualism, since others in my class were strengthened in their faith through their studies" (my paraphrase of his words).[20]

IS IT JUST A MATTER OF HUMAN OPINION?

I continued my article with this: "But here's the thing. Just because there are different opinions as to how to translate a biblical verse doesn't mean that the original author was ambiguous in his writing, even if we debate the meaning today."

In other words, just because we have differences on a subject doesn't mean the truth is up for grabs. Not at all. As I wrote:

> And just because Jewish translators of the Bible render certain key words one way and Christian translators render those same words another way doesn't mean that one translation is not ultimately better than the other.
>
> In the same way, just because Hindus conceive of the Godhead in a polytheistic way while Jews, Christians,

and Muslims conceive of the Godhead in different monotheistic ways doesn't mean that all these competing ideologies are equally true. God is who He is, regardless of what we think or believe.

Just look at our political views today. Or our views on moral and cultural and social issues.

The fact that we are deeply divided doesn't mean that all sides are equally right. And the fact that our presuppositions color our worldview doesn't mean that all presuppositions are equally valid (or invalid).[21]

In short, "When it comes to the Bible, we do not read it in a vacuum, nor did the authors of the Scripture write it in a vacuum." This is a very important point. As I explained:

To give one example, the disciples of Jesus knew that His interpretation of the Bible was true because they saw it with their own eyes. They heard Him say that He would be rejected and crucified. They heard Him say that He would rise from the dead. And they heard Him say, "It is all written in our Bible in advance!"

Then, after His crucifixion and resurrection, when He pointed back to the Hebrew Bible and said, "It's all predicted here!" their eyes were opened. There it was, in black and white, written centuries in advance by the prophets. (See Luke 24:13–49.) That settled things, forever. Who could possibly convince them otherwise?

In my case, my life was undeniably transformed by Jesus the Messiah. And, over the last 50 years, I could point to countless examples of God's reality in my life (and the lives of those I'm close with). In fact, I would have to shut off my mind to deny my faith. In the words of the bestselling book by Norman Geisler and Frank Turek, *I Don't Have Enough Faith to Be an Atheist*.

But that doesn't mean that I didn't wrestle with intellectual arguments and questions of biblical interpretation. To the contrary, I wrestled deeply, and to this day, I'm engaging these questions and challenges.

Yet what I can say [is] this: My studies confirmed my beliefs. And should I have a question about which theological system is correct, my experience in God tells me which theology is right.[22]

There is, then, a "beautiful loop" of seeking Him with all our hearts and studying about Him with all our minds. The two go hand in hand, each one complementing and strengthening the other. As I expressed in the article:

> So, there is a beautiful, continuous loop, one in which the truth of Scripture is confirmed through experience, and as that truth is shared with others, they too experience God for themselves. And as we dig deeper in study, we find answers to our deepest questions.
>
> Again, to be clear, I do not sit in judgment of "Phanatik." To the contrary, my heart goes out to him.
>
> But I will say this to everyone struggling with his or her faith. G. K. Chesterton once wrote, "The Christian ideal has not been tried and found wanting. It has been found difficult; and left untried."
>
> And for many, that is the key. The Scriptures say repeatedly that God rewards those who diligently seek Him, who search for Him and His truth more than a miner searches for gold and silver (see, e.g., Deuteronomy 4:29; Jeremiah 29:13; Proverbs 3:13–18; Luke 18:1–8; Hebrews 11:6). We are to seek Him with heart *and* mind, spirit *and* intellect.

Yet the fact is that very few of us really seek God and His truth this earnestly—by which I do not mean simply studying but rather literally seeking Him in prayer and fasting day and night until we encounter Him. I mean crying out to Him for reality and truth and encounter as if our very life depended on it.

If we will do that, refusing to quit or give up until a breakthrough comes, He *will* reveal Himself and He *will* confirm the truth of His Word. He cannot deny Himself.[23]

In the pages that follow, we will probe some difficult, honest questions. And we will not shy away from posing difficult, honest answers. As you journey with me, you will be journeying with someone who is 100 percent sure—with every fiber of my being, with all my heart and soul, all my intellect and spirit—that the God of the Bible is real, that the Scriptures are His Word, and that Jesus is Lord. From that firm foundation I ask the fundamental question from which this book draws its title: Why have so many Christians left the faith? Let's get some answers together.

CHAPTER 2

ATHEISTS, AGNOSTICS, AND THE TRICKLE-DOWN EFFECT

So many Christians are leaving the faith today, in particular those who once identified as evangelicals, that a new term has been coined to describe them: exvangelicals! According to Wikipedia:

> Exvangelical is a social movement of people who have left evangelicalism, especially white evangelical churches in the United States, for atheism, agnosticism, progressive Christianity, or any other religious belief. The hashtag #exvangelical was coined by Blake Chastain in 2016 to make "a safe space for people to find solidarity with others who have gone through similar experiences."[1]

Chastain also started a podcast titled *Exvangelical,* and there are other popular exvangelical podcasts, such as *Almost Heretical* and *Straight White American Jesus.*

Could it be, then, that we are now in the time of the final apostasy, a time of which both Jesus and Paul spoke?[2] Could this be the final falling away? Personally, I do not believe that we are in that final time of apostasy. But without question I can say that this is the most significant falling away I have ever witnessed, and numerous factors are contributing to this current crisis of faith. We will examine them one by one in the chapters that follow, starting right here and now.

THE ALL-OUT ASSAULT ON GOD AND THE BIBLE

Josh McDowell is one of the best-known Christian apologists of our times, author of modern classics such as *Evidence That Demands a Verdict* and *More Than a Carpenter*, with more than 150 books written or coauthored in 128 languages. According to his bio, "Since 1960, Josh has delivered more than 27,000 talks to over 25,000,000 people in 125 countries."[3] This man has been around.

A few years ago we were speaking at an apologetics conference together when he made the striking comment that the objections he used to run into on college campuses he's now hearing from kids who are twelve or thirteen years old.

His words are very disturbing to hear since they mean kids who are middle school age and younger are getting exposed to college-level objections, objections most of them are not ready to process in an emotionally mature and intellectually sophisticated manner. So at an impressionable age they're getting hit with anti-God memes and anti-Bible themes, all of which sow seeds of doubt and skepticism into their hearts. In many cases, their parents or Christian educators probably have no idea this is happening.

These kids are hearing that the Bible can't be trusted. That God is a fairy tale. That Christians are hateful. That the church is for the older generation. That religion is make-believe. In short, *it's time we move on from all this, especially if you want to be "cool" and "in."*

All these young people have to do is like the comment or copy the meme or share the video, and before you know it, the message has gone viral. No need to think about it. No need to process it. No need to debate it. Just pass it on, and let peer pressure and peer momentum do the rest.

It's tough enough when college and university students get exposed to serious objections to their faith. Who are they to argue with their professors? What makes them right—after all, they're just students—and their lecturers wrong? And didn't their pastor always seem a little simplistic and naive? But when younger kids get hit with these same objections, they often absorb them without much thought. And if the other kids are mocking, you certainly don't want to become the object of their scorn. Better to join the crowd.

How, then, did these objections trickle down to these young people? How have they become so pervasive on our university campuses, not to mention in the culture as a whole?

THE RISE OF THE NEW ATHEISTS

The year 2006 marks the rise of what has been called the new atheism, the year when a number of outspoken, aggressive atheists became best-selling authors. Looking back from the vantage point of 2019, an article in the UK's *The Guardian* noted that the new atheism was born in the febrile aftermath of 9/11, when belief in a deity—or, let's be honest, specifically in Allah—seemed to some people a newly urgent danger to western civilisation. Sam Harris began writing *The End of Faith* (2004) immediately after the World Trade Center attacks, and it became a bestseller. There followed the philosopher Daniel Dennett's *Breaking the Spell*, Richard Dawkins's *The God Delusion*, and Christopher Hitchens's *God Is Not Great*.[4]

The books by Dennett and Dawkins were published in 2006, while Hitchens' book was published in 2007. All of these books, whose authors became known as the Four Horsemen of the New Atheism, received national—and even international—attention. Harris' book was on the *New York Times* best-seller list for thirty-three weeks. Dennett's volume stirred up a firestorm of criticism and reaction.[5] By 2010, Dawkins reported total sales of *more than two million books*,[6] while in 2014 he claimed the number had surpassed *three million*.[7] Not to be outdone, Hitchens' book "was published on May 1, 2007, and within a week had reached No. 2 on the Amazon bestsellers list (behind *Harry Potter and the Deathly Hallows*), and reached No. 1 on the *New York Times Bestseller* list in its third week."[8]

Atheism was in the air, and there was nothing subtle about it, as the titles and subtitles of their books make clear:

- *The End of Faith: Religion, Terror, and the Future of Reason*

- *Breaking the Spell: Religion as a Natural Phenomenon*

- *The God Delusion*—actually, this one had no subtitle; the title said it all.

- *God Is Not Great: How Religion Poisons Everything*

In Harris' words, "Most religions have merely canonized a few products of ancient ignorance and derangement and passed them down to us as though they were primordial truths. This leaves billions of us believing what no sane person could believe on his own."[9] In short, you'd have to be crazy to be a deeply religious person. That's why Dennett could say, "There's simply no polite way to tell people they've dedicated their lives to an illusion."[10] Best, then, to be blunt about it and wake people up from their religious dream.

Dawkins pulled no punches, claiming that "faith is the great cop-out, the great excuse to evade the need to think and evaluate evidence. Faith is belief in spite of, even perhaps because of, the lack of evidence."[11] In other words, no one with a working brain would ever believe what you believe. Hitchens seconded this. He wrote, "Gullibility and credulity are considered undesirable qualities in every department of human life—except religion....Why are we praised by godly men for surrendering our 'godly gift' of reason when we cross their mental thresholds?"[12] Accordingly, the only way you could believe in the Bible or the God of the Bible (or any other religious faith and book) was by saying no to reason and yes to gullibility. The matter was either-or.

As for the God of the Bible in particular, the God of the Old Testament, Dawkins was even more direct: "The God of the Old Testament is arguably the most unpleasant character in all fiction: jealous and proud of it; a petty, unjust, unforgiving control-freak; a vindictive, bloodthirsty ethnic cleanser; a misogynistic, homophobic, racist, infanticidal, genocidal, filicidal, pestilential, megalomaniacal, sadomasochistic, capriciously malevolent bully."[13] Atheist activist and former evangelical Dan Barker turned this quote into a book titled *God: The Most Unpleasant Character in All Fiction*.[14] Dawkins provided fresh fuel for Barker's anti-God fire.

As for the alleged positive benefits of religious faith, according to Hitchens, "We keep on being told that religion, whatever its imperfections, at least instills morality. On every side, there is conclusive evidence that the contrary is the case and that faith causes people to be more mean, more selfish, and perhaps above all, more stupid."[15] Best, then, to get rid of religious faith, get rid of this idea of God, get rid of the Bible, along with other outdated myths and fables, and get on with *real* life. In fact, if you are a thinking person—or simply want to be regarded as a thinking person—that is the only reasonable thing to do.

Of course, aggressive atheistic arguments are nothing new, with men like Bertrand Russell (1872–1970) popularizing them long before the so-called Four Horsemen. And many other prominent, eloquent, outspoken atheists came before and after him. But when the books of a number of atheists, most of them quite aggressive in tone and quite articulate in speech, become national best sellers, their arguments hit the fan, so to say, resulting in the rapid spread of their ideas, jumping from the intelligentsia to the person on the street.

Interestingly, it was also in 2006 that Josh McDowell's *The Last Christian Generation* was published. He wrote, "The Christian faith has been under attack in this culture for decades and because most believers haven't been equipped to know what they believe, the very foundation of Christianity within the Church has eroded. If trends continue, the next generation of the Church will not even be rightfully called Christian."[16] Talk about a prescient warning.

Make no mistake, the new atheists were looking for new converts, functioning as evangelists of unbelief and apostles of cynicism and doubt. And they were shaking up lots of people who were being exposed to these arguments for the first time in their lives. Or do you think it was a coincidence that by the end of 2006 "The Blasphemy Challenge" started trending online? As explained on the Got Questions website:

> The "blasphemy challenge" is an internet-based project started in December 2006 which invites young people to submit videos to Youtube [sic] or other video internet hosts, in which they record themselves blaspheming or denying the existence of the Holy Spirit. The first 1001 users who took the blasphemy challenge were sent a DVD of [Brian] Flemming's film "The God Who Wasn't There."[17]
>
> The website went on to say that "celebrity atheists such as Christopher Hitchens, Daniel Dennett, and Penn Jillette participated in the project," a product of a group called the Rational Response Squad.[18]

This was not simply a matter of losing one's faith. This was about actively rejecting God and the Bible to the point of mocking Him and His Word. People of all ages joined in the challenge, including little children who clearly had no idea what they were saying. It was a painful thing to watch.

Over time, then, through the influence of these books (and others), through the popularizing of atheistic arguments, through viral videos, and through social media, this hostility to God and the Bible trickled down to the larger society until the same people who had no idea when the Bronze Age took place could refer to the Lord as a Bronze Age god and the Bible as a Bronze Age book. Who needs any of *that stuff* in the twenty-first century?

As I wrote in 2017:

> It is popular these days to attack the Bible as an evil book and to malign the God of the Bible as an evil god. We are told that the Scriptures are outdated, outmoded, out of touch, and outlandish. Internet mockers and atheistic authors assure us that "the Bible [specifically, the Old Testament] was written by a bunch of Bronze Age goat herders" or penned by "Bronze Age desert tribesmen," and so it is as irrelevant socially and morally as it is sci-entifically....As someone posted on my Facebook page, "I like how you think your outdated bronze-age mythology is relevant. That's too cute."[19]

WHEN SCHOLARLY OBJECTIONS BECOME MAINSTREAMED

It was not just the aggressive objections of the new atheists that trickled down to the larger population, including young people. It was also the objections of agnostic biblical scholars like Bart Ehrman, the James A. Gray Distinguished Professor in the Department of Religious Studies at the University of North Carolina, Chapel Hill, and a respected New Testament scholar. Some of his books, which cast doubt on the reliability of the New Testament, especially the Gospels, became major best sellers, to the surprise of everyone involved. Whoever dreamed that books like this would sell that well? Not Professor Ehrman, and not his publisher. But sell they did, and once again, for the first time, many Christians were confronted with challenges for which they had no answers. And when did he release the first of these books? November 2005, just two months before 2006. I'm speaking of *Misquoting Jesus: The Story Behind Who Changed the Bible and Why.*[20]

Of great interest is that Christian scholars had been aware of these issues for decades—in some cases, for centuries—and had solid responses for each and every question that Ehrman raised. For them, there was nothing new in these books nor anything to challenge our faith.

To be sure, thousands of New Testament manuscripts contain tens of thousands of contradictions between them. This leads many to wonder: How, then, can we trust our Bibles today? How can we tell which manuscript is accurate and which is not?

For biblical scholars, this was an old question that was answered long ago, and rather than looking at these thousands of manuscripts in a negative light, this should be seen as a massive plus. In other words, *the New Testament is, by far, the best-preserved book written in the ancient Greco-Roman world.* There is not even a close second. As noted by F. F. Bruce, one of the greatest biblical scholars of the last century, "The evidence for our New Testament writings is ever so much greater than the evidence for many writings of classical authors, the authenticity of which no one dreams of questioning. And if the New Testament were a collection of secular writings, their authenticity would generally be regarded as beyond all doubt."[21]

More recently, professor James Prothro, who earned his PhD from the University of Cambridge, noted that when compared with other ancient manuscripts from famous works of the past, "the New Testament still has earlier relative attestation, more extensive attestation, and far fewer chronological gaps from the time of composition and the time of the printing press and modern editions....Indeed, noted classicist Giorgio Pasquali has said as much of the New Testament: 'No other Greek text is handed down so richly and credibly.'"[22]

Professor Daniel Wallace, a world-respected expert in the transmission of the Greek New Testament text, puts it like this:

> How high do you think the stack of New Testament manuscripts would be? Think about this: of just the 5,800+ Greek New Testament manuscripts, there are more than 2.6 million pages. Combining both the Old and New Testament, there are more than 66,000 manuscripts and scrolls. A stack of extant manuscripts for the average classical writer would measure about four feet high; this just cannot compare to the more than one mile of New Testament manuscripts and two-and-a-half-miles for the entire Bible.[23]

Some fragmentary manuscripts can be dated as early as one century after the time of Jesus, something that is absolutely unprecedented in terms of the preservation of ancient records and historical accounts. The Lord really took care to preserve His Word!

As for the contradictions, the vast majority of them are extremely minor, the equivalent of a difference between a comma and semicolon in English today, or between spelling Mr. versus Mister. Plus, New Testament scholars who focus on these issues (known as textual critics) use scientific methods to help determine which readings are the most accurate. Based on meticulous, scholarly studies, translators then render these words into English for us to read. When you take out a good English translation of the Bible, you can feel confident that what you are reading is accurate, especially if you compare multiple translations and see that, in every case, the overall sense of the words is the same.

Not only so, but in most modern Bibles, some of the very questions Ehrman raised are found right in the footnotes of the Bibles we read every day (such as the question of the validity of John 8:1–11, the passage about the woman caught in adultery). It's just that most of us don't bother to read those notes—and if we use digital or audio Bibles, we never even see the notes.

That's why for many Christians these questions didn't arise until they read Ehrman's books: *Can I really trust my Bible? Can I be sure that Jesus really said these things? Is this really the Word of God after all?* Unfortunately, while more than two million copies of Ehrman's books were reportedly sold, the books written by Christian scholars responding to Ehrman were sold in the thousands, meaning that the questions went out widely but the answers did not.

Again, any graduate from a solid seminary would have encountered these issues and been given tools with which to respond. But your average Bible reader had no idea such tools existed, and now, for the first time, they faced a tidal wave of objections and challenges. No wonder so many lost their way. In addition, since they first heard these objections from non-believers like Ehrman, many felt as if their spiritual leaders had been hiding something from them or as if Christian scholars were part of some great conspiracy to cover up the truth about the Bible. "They've been lying to us all these years! It's all part of the religious establishment. It's all about power and control and money." And so the seeds of doubt were sown deeply into many hearts and minds.

We could even factor in here things like Dan Brown's novel *The Da Vinci Code*, one of the best-selling books of all time. In it, Brown claimed that Mary Magdalene was the wife of Jesus and that their offspring remain until this day. The book was so well written and gave the appearance of being so well researched that many people believed it to be true, even though it was fiction. This too added to the overall mistrust in the Scriptures, giving the feeling of "my leaders haven't been honest with me. They're hiding the real truth. It's a big religious conspiracy meant to keep us in the dark!" In many ways, it was a perfect storm.

How, then, do we respond? And how do we help those who lost their way? For those with questions about the trustworthiness of the Bible, I have listed some very helpful resources in the appendix. As for the so-called new atheism and its attacks on the God of the Bible, let's address that here and now.

THE FAILURE OF THE NEW ATHEISM

The mocking swagger of the new atheism that confused and unnerved so many has also been part of its demise. That's because, when you so aggressively attack faith in God, ridiculing those who believe in Him and mocking the Bible, you set yourself up for a fall. The moment the weaknesses of your own position are exposed—be it philosophically, morally, or scientifically—your whole house of cards begins to collapse.

For example, an article on the *Psychology Today* website called out Richard Dawkins for being inconsistent on the question of free will. Philosophy professor Tamler Sommers wrote the article titled "Can an Atheist Believe in Free Will?" Sommers referenced a five-minute video "accusing Richard Dawkins of being inconsistent in holding that belief in free will and moral responsibility is justified but that belief in God is unjustified."

Sommers explained, "Dawkins concedes that if you take a deterministic or mechanistic view of the universe, it seems absurd to think we have free will and that we can go around blaming criminals and praising distinguished authors" but that Dawkins concludes that "this is an inconsistency we have to live with" and so we may continue to believe in free will and moral responsibility, and blame and praise people accordingly. (In his defense, he does seem slightly uncomfortable about the tension.)[24]

How interesting. The learned professor Dawkins must admit to being inconsistent here. But of course he must. After all, how can there be blame and praise when the process of evolution has locked everything into place? As expressed by Pastor J. D. Greear, "If all we are is biology and chemistry, then our behavior in any situation is solely due to what our genes and chemicals in us compel us to choose. Even when we think we're acting freely, it's only because some chemical construct in our minds pushes us to act that way, because there is no 'us' behind it all. There is only our flesh."[25]

In fact, if atheist philosopher Daniel Dennett is correct, then even the sense of consciousness that you experience (as in, "I think, therefore I am") is an illusion. As he famously wrote, "What we think of as our consciousness is actually our brains pulling a number of tricks to conjure up the world as we experience it. But in reality, it's all smoke, mirrors, and rapidly firing neurons."[26]

As explained by Anna Buckley on BBC News:

> From an evolutionary perspective, our ability to think is no different from our ability to digest, says Dennett. Both these biological activities can be explained by Darwin's Theory of Natural Selection, often described as the survival of the fittest. We evolved from uncomprehending bacteria. Our minds, with all their remarkable talents, are the result of endless biological experiments. Our genius is not God-given. It's the result of millions of years of trial and error.[27]

In the words of Steven Pinker, a psychology professor at Harvard and an outspoken atheist, "Computation has finally demystified mentalistic terms. Beliefs are inscriptions in memory, desires are goal inscriptions, thinking is computation, perceptions are inscriptions triggered by sensors, trying is executing operations triggered by a goal."[28] Or, we might add, even feelings of love can be reduced to a mathematical process in the brain.

Now, as an atheist, you might not accept all these arguments. But you must, to be consistent, accept some of them. Does that bring you a sense of hope or a sense of despair? What of the fact that, without a God who can intervene, whichever way the world is going, it will continue to go? Nothing can change or alter that. How does that make you feel?[29]

Dawkins also found himself in the midst of intense controversy because of statements he made in 2014. As reported by *The Independent* in May 2021:

> While speaking to RTE presenter Brendan O'Connor recently, Dawkins was challenged about an exchange

he had in 2014, where he told a Twitter user who mentioned the "ethical dilemma" of having a baby with Down's Syndrome, that they should: "Abort it and try again. It would be immoral to bring it into the world if you have the choice."

Although Dawkins admitted that he had put his view "a bit too strongly," he doubled down by saying: "It seems to me to be plausible that you probably would increase the amount of happiness in the world more by having another child instead [of one with a disability]."[30]

This is where his atheism led him. Away with Down's syndrome babies! The world would be much better without them (and this way, no more Down's syndrome children or adults in the future). That's what happens when you don't recognize each human being as created in the image of God. That's what happens when "survival of the fittest" is the evolutionary rule.

So Dawkins is criticized for being inconsistent with his atheism (blaming and praising people as if they truly had free will) and for being consistent with his atheism (and saying the world would be better without disabled people).

No wonder, then, that in 2004 Alister McGrath, who holds three doctorates from Oxford University, published his book *The Twilight of Atheism: The Rise and Fall of Disbelief in the Modern World*.[31] Looking at the worldwide picture, atheism was actually on the decline, not the rise. Accordingly, in 2015 the late sociologist Rodney Stark published his book *The Triumph of Faith: Why the World Is More Religious Than Ever*.[32] Little surprise, then, that the Conservapedia website could announce that "2021 is the WORST year in the history of atheism."[33] And no wonder that, also in 2021, radio host Eric Metaxas published his book *Is Atheism Dead?*[34] Atheism simply doesn't deliver the goods, especially during times of crisis and hardship. That's because atheism doesn't *have* the goods.

In fact, while some atheists might boast of their personal strength—as in, "I don't need God to live a productive life"—and mock religious believers as people who need some kind of crutch, at many times in life we *do* need a crutch (and more!). That's why you will often hear testimonies declaring, "I was a drug addict for thirty years, and Jesus set me free," or "Our marriage was on the rocks, and we cried out to God, and He saved our marriage," or "The doctors gave our little girl three weeks to live, and the people in our church prayed around the clock, and our little girl was totally healed. That was twenty-five years ago, and she just had her third child today!" Atheism does none of that.

Additionally, during those agonizingly dark times, when believers suffer calamity and hardship like everyone else, losing a child to a freak accident or getting raped or being betrayed by a close friend or going bankrupt or experiencing divorce, it is the very real presence of God that carries them through. An atheist can only rely on personal fortitude and the help of other people since "there is no God to deliver or help or heal." Yet countless tens of millions of believers today can testify that His presence at such times is absolutely real.

As for when God intervenes miraculously, especially with medically documented healings, atheism can offer no explanation other than to point to all the times when God does not heal, as if to say, "If God is so good and so powerful, why doesn't He heal the others?" That, of course, is a fair question, but the reality is that healing is not guaranteed in every situation for every person.[35] But that question does not negate the reality of divine healing, a reality that is becoming increasingly well documented. In fact, it takes more "faith" to deny the reality of these miracles or to try to explain them away than to believe in their existence as loving acts of a powerful God.

Ironically, in the end the new atheists simply created their own religion, but one that could not possibly compare with the reality of having a personal relationship with God. As noted in *The Guardian*, "In its messianic conviction that it alone serves the cause of truth, this too is a faith as noxious as any other."[36]

THE INSIGHT THAT HELPED LIBERATE C. S. LEWIS FROM ATHEISM

C. S. Lewis (1898–1963) was perhaps the greatest Christian apologist of the twentieth century along with being a noted scholar in English literature. But Lewis was first an atheist, and in his mind, he had an airtight argument against God. He explained:

> If a good God made the world why has it gone wrong? And for many years I simply refused to listen to the Christian answers to this question, because I kept on feeling "whatever you say, and however clever your arguments are, isn't it much simpler and easier to say that the world was not made by any intelligent power? Aren't all your arguments simply a complicated attempt to avoid the obvious?" But then that threw me back into another difficulty.

So these Christians had a counterargument to his argument, and in the end he found it compelling. He wrote:

> My argument against God was that the universe seemed so cruel and unjust. But how had I got this idea of just and unjust? A man does not call a line crooked unless he has some idea of a straight line. What was I comparing this universe with when I called it unjust?...Thus in the very act of trying to prove that God did not exist—in other words, that the whole of reality was senseless—I found I was forced to assume that one part of reality—namely my idea of justice—was full of sense. Consequently atheism turns out to be too simple. If the whole universe has no meaning, we should never have found out that it has no meaning: just as, if there were no light in the universe and therefore no creatures with eyes, we should never know it was dark. *Dark* would be without meaning.[37]

Note carefully those words: "Consequently atheism turns out to be too simple." He nailed it on the head. One of my colleagues, Frank Turek, wrote a book titled *Stealing From God*. The subtitle says it all: *Why Atheists Need God to Make Their Case*.[38]

And for all the atheistic claims that Darwinian evolution solves the puzzle of human existence, it actually does no such thing. As expressed by David Gelernter, a famous Yale University computer science professor, "The origin of species is exactly what Darwin *cannot* explain." As he writes: "Like so many others, I grew up with Darwin's theory, and had always believed it was true. I had heard doubts over the years from well-informed, sometimes brilliant people, but I had my hands full cultivating my garden, and it was easier to let biology take care of itself. But in recent years, reading and discussion have shut that road down for good."[39]

Back in 2012 Thomas Nagel, a highly respected philosophy professor, released a book titled *Mind & Cosmos*, published by Oxford University Press. In the book, Nagel, an atheist, expresses his strong doubts about Darwinian naturalism, writing, "I realize that such doubts will strike many people as outrageous, but that is because almost everyone in our secular culture has been browbeaten into regarding the reductive research program as sacrosanct, on the ground that anything else would not be science."

And although he did not like the conclusions he was coming to, seeing that he was an atheist, he had to be honest with these doubts:

> For a long time I have found the materialist account of how we and our fellow organisms came to exist hard to believe, including the standard version of how the evolutionary process works. The more details we learn about the chemical basis of life and the intricacy of the genetic code, the more unbelievable the standard historical account becomes. This is just the opinion of a layman who reads widely in the literature that explains contemporary science to the nonspecialist. Perhaps that literature presents the situation with a simplicity and confidence that does not reflect the most sophisticated scientific thought in these areas. But it seems to me that, as it is usually presented, the current orthodoxy about the cosmic order is the product of governing assumptions that are unsupported, and that it flies in the face of common sense.[40]

Could it be, then, that the atheists have their sets of assumptions, their dogmas, their leaps of faith? Absolutely! Could it be that they too deal with peer pressure and prevailing orthodoxies? Without question. That's why Frank Turek, along with the renowned apologist Norman Geisler, wrote the best-selling book I referenced in the first chapter, *I Don't Have Enough Faith to Be an Atheist*.[41] As theologian R. C. Sproul writes: "The New Testament maintains that unbelief is generated not so much by intellectual causes as by moral and psychological ones. The problem is not that there is insufficient evidence to convince rational beings that there is a God, but that rational beings have a natural hostility to the being of God."[42] Note that Sproul is not speaking so much of the unbelief that comes through loss, disappointment, and pain but the unbelief that comes through hardening the heart.

In the end, atheism is not sustainable, as people who don't believe in God simply find new things to believe in (including the most bizarre superstitions), and countries like Albania, which at one time proclaimed itself to be atheistic, can only suppress religious faith for so long. As noted in a 2007 article, "Albania became the first officially atheist country in the world in 1967. Its ruler, Enver Hoxha, ordered all churches and mosques demolished or converted into sports arenas, warehouses or other secular facilities. He shut the borders. And until communism collapsed in 1990, public expressions of faith were banned."[43]

Fast-forward another twenty years: "According to Albania's 2011 census, 58.79% of the population are Muslim, while Christians account for 16.92% of the population. Atheists and non-affiliated believers make up 2.5% and 5.49% of the population, respectively. 13.79% of the population preferred not to answer the question in the census related to religion."[44] Note that both Muslim and Christian religious leaders felt the figures from their respective groups were too low. So after banning all religious expression in the country, in the end only 2.5 percent of the population professed atheism.

The simple truth is that God is and forever will be. Of that, you can be sure. In fact, you can stake your life on it.

CHAPTER 3

CAN CHRISTIAN LEADERS BE TRUSTED?

I F YOU HAVE read the Bible, you know that leaders can fall. And if you understand human nature, you realize that no one is untouchable and that all of us have the capacity to blow it badly, often to the shock of those close to us. "I can't believe he (or she) did that!" At the same time, the Bible is very clear that ministry leaders are to be examples, to be "above reproach," to have a "good reputation with outsiders," to be morally disciplined and spiritually sound. (We'll look at some New Testament requirements for leaders later in this chapter.) We *should* expect better of them, shouldn't we?

After all, the Christian message is that Jesus not only forgives but that He also transforms, making us into "new creations" in Christ. (See 2 Corinthians 5:17.) This applies all the more to those in leadership positions. They, above all, should be living examples of the transformative power of the gospel, able to say to their people, "Follow me, as I follow the

Messiah."[1] But if so many of them are falling, what does that say about their Savior? Is He unable to keep them? Does the gospel really work?

Some have concluded, "People are going to do what they do. You can't blame the Lord for their decisions. But this is why I have left the church. *I don't trust people, especially leaders.* That's my issue. These Christian leaders have given me very little reason to trust them anytime soon."

Truth be told, it would be one thing if we heard about a scandal involving a major church leader once in a blue moon. The exception would prove the rule: these are godly men and women who are true to their faith and whose lives point people to the Lord. That's why it is so rare to see any of them fall.

But these days it feels as if the reverse is true. Scandals feel like they're a dime a dozen. Who will be the next famous minister to be exposed for some kind of sexual sin or financial corruption or other kind of moral failure? Which Christian group will be next?

On the Protestant side, one day it's a beloved apologist[2] or the president of a Christian university.[3] Another day it's a celebrity pastor,[4] then it's that pastor's related network of churches,[5] then a whole denomination.[6] On the Catholic side, one devastating report from France, with research dating back to the 1950s, documented 330,000 cases of ministry-related sex abuse.[7] How many millions did this affect? "If that's Christianity," many think to themselves (or perhaps say out loud), "then I want nothing to do with it."

To be clear, I do not write this to pour salt into the wounds of those who have sinned and fallen. The old saying "there but for the grace of God go I" has never been truer. But we cannot deny reality. Our reputation as followers of Jesus has been stained, deeply so. Worse still, we have made our Savior look bad. That is a very serious issue.

ALL OF US HATE HYPOCRISY

Think about it for a moment. Let's say you were hired by a health company that specialized in natural products that were reported to work almost miraculously. At least that's what the company claimed, and it seemed to have the success to prove it. Plus, the founders and leaders of the company were living proof that the products work, having used them themselves for many years. Just look at how healthy they are!

How would you feel, then, if you discovered that these leaders were living a lie? That they were all sick with debilitating conditions, the long-term, negative side effects of their alleged wonder products? That those few leaders who were not sick had stopped using their own product years ago and had resorted to traditional Western medicines and treatments?

How long would you stay with this company? How long would your conscience allow you to keep making money by selling snake oil to the gullible public? Wouldn't you want to expose this for all the world to see?

Or what if you joined a company known for its integrity, hailed nationwide for its high moral standards, its fair treatment of all employees, and its generosity to the local communities wherever it operated? Surely you would be excited to work with such an upstanding group. Surely this was a dream environment for a hardworking employee. Surely you could stay there for years.

Except the company was not what it was cracked up to be. It was all smoke and mirrors, all a façade. Massive corruption existed at the top. Employees were taken advantage of, then intimidated into silence. And the company's apparent "generosity" was nothing more than a sham since they overcharged their customers to generate much more profit, sending a little back to make them look good. How would you feel about that company now?

We could think about endless examples like this, but in each case if the product we were selling really didn't work or if all the positives of the company or organization were just a charade, unless we too were corrupt, we would be out the door in a heartbeat. Really now, would you follow someone on a dangerous jungle trail if they had no idea where they were going? Would you read a book filled with insights on how to fight depression after learning the author had killed himself out of despair? Would you follow the healthy diet plan of an obese cook?

How much more, then, when it comes to God, to the Bible, to the gospel, to Jesus? How much more when it comes to people who preach against sin yet are secretly living in it? Who tell the world, "You need to repent!" while they themselves practice those same things? The very expression "Practice what you preach" says it all.

We expect preachers to be different from others—at least, we used to. We expect people who are entrusted with sacred work to emulate morality and godliness. We expect people with the title "Reverend" before their names to live reverent lives.

A Christian friend of mine recently told me about one of his coworkers who was unusually resistant to the gospel. One day my friend found out his story. When he was a little boy living in Italy, on two separate occasions, he found the local Catholic priest having sex with a woman (in fact, a different woman each time). Once, it was in an empty field near the boy's house, and another time it was in the priest's own home (the boy's mother had insisted he bring some food to the priest at a time he was not expecting visitors). That was it for this kid. From that day on, he did not believe. Who can fault him? "So much for religion!"

Back in 2006, one of the nation's most respected evangelical leaders, a man with access to the White House, a pastor openly opposed to same-sex "marriage" legislation in his state, got caught in a major scandal. He was using meth and having sex with a male prostitute. Yes, the man who helped lead his state's opposition to gay "marriage" was himself engaging in gay sex. While married to his wife. While pastoring a megachurch. While speaking out for morality in the nation.

It was only when the prostitute saw him on TV and realized he spoke out against gay relationships that he decided to go public with his charges. And so a gay male prostitute came out as the moral champion in the story and a national evangelical leader came out as the immoral hypocrite.[8]

Again, I do not write this to condemn or to mock. The fact is that none of us have any idea where we would be today if the Lord's grace was lifted from our lives. It really is a terrifying thought.

But I do write this to say that I understand why these scandals have been so devastating. I understand how they have driven sincere people out of the church. (All the more is this true when they themselves were victims of sexual abuse, and rather than church leaders helping them and disciplining those who sinned, they blamed the victims and protected the guilty. How the Lord must hate all this!) I understand how these failings—so many of them, in so many different Christian groups and organizations—cause people to mistrust

Christian leaders, or their message or their God or all of the above. Yet here too, there is more to the story.

JESUS DIDN'T FAIL

Although at first glance what I'm about to say may seem like a convenient theological cop-out, it is absolutely true: people may have failed—influential people with spiritual authority and power—but Jesus didn't fail. To the contrary, He died for our failings, pouring out grace and offering forgiveness. *And He will judge us for abusing that grace.* But to repeat, it is not the Lord who failed.

In the Hebrew and Greek languages, the same word is used for *pastor* and for *shepherd.* That means that Jesus the Great Shepherd is also Jesus the Great Pastor. It also means that every pastor is a shepherd responsible for the Lord's sheep. Be assured that He is jealous for each and every lamb! That's why He gave His disciples this warning:

> Watch out for false prophets. They come to you in sheep's clothing, but inwardly they are ferocious wolves. By their fruit you will recognize them. Do people pick grapes from thornbushes, or figs from thistles? Likewise, every good tree bears good fruit, but a bad tree bears bad fruit. A good tree cannot bear bad fruit, and a bad tree cannot bear good fruit. Every tree that does not bear good fruit is cut down and thrown into the fire. Thus, by their fruit you will recognize them.
> —MATTHEW 7:15–20

Paul issued a similar warning to a group of elders he had mentored and trained, speaking to them with great passion during the last hours they had together. He said:

> Now I know that none of you among whom I have gone about preaching the kingdom will ever see me again. Therefore, I declare to you today that I am innocent of the blood of any of you. For I have not hesitated to proclaim to you the whole will of God. Keep watch over yourselves and all the flock of which the Holy Spirit has made you overseers. Be shepherds of the church of God, which he bought with his own blood. I know that after I leave, savage wolves will come in among you and will not spare the flock. Even from your own number men will arise and distort the truth in order to draw away disciples after them. So be on your guard! Remember that for three years I never stopped warning each of you night and day with tears.
>
> —Acts 20:25–31

Notice in particular these words: "Be shepherds of the church of God, which he bought with his own blood." Jesus paid the ultimate price for His sheep—for you and for me—and He expects the pastors, His appointed shepherds, to do their jobs well. This is a matter of life and death.

And notice how strongly both Jesus and Paul warn about these ferocious and savage wolves who will infiltrate the flocks. Watch yourselves as leaders, says Paul, and watch yourselves as believers, says Jesus. Danger lies ahead!

Can we, then, blame Jesus if we are negligent and let one of these wolves bite us? Can we blame Paul if one of these leaders fails to do his duty? Obviously not. Jesus and Paul did everything they could to stop the bleeding before it even happened. Others failed in their mission and let the wolves come in (or, worse still, became wolves themselves).

"But," you say, "that's the whole problem. God is God, and

He could have stopped these wolves from touching us at all. I was just an innocent sheep, trusting my pastor. Little did I know that he was a sexual predator."

To be perfectly candid, I cannot relate to what you lived through, and perhaps I would have lost all faith in God had I experienced this same kind of deep spiritual, emotional, and physical trauma. But I can say this: because God gave us free will, He allows evil things to happen every moment of every day. He doesn't stop every drunk driver from hitting innocent victims. He doesn't stop every abusive husband from beating his wife. He doesn't stop every despondent woman from aborting her baby. He doesn't stop every madman from declaring war. And He doesn't stop you from leaving Him. Or denying Him. Or cursing Him. Or mocking Him. Or running back into His arms.

Almighty God, the Maker of heaven and earth, gave us free wills, urging us to choose life but not forcing us to. Yet because He is God, in the midst of our human sin and rebellion and failing, He works out His will, bringing joy, freedom, healing, and redemption. The sooner you realize that He is not your enemy, that He is not the one who abused you, that He grieved for you and with you as you suffered pain and shame, and that He is here to help you and restore you even now, the sooner your life will turn for the better.

Jesus the Great Shepherd *will* take care of His sheep, and if you will simply confess to Him (even by faith), "Lord, I know You didn't fail me," your healing can begin. Multiplied millions have found this to be true.

But to say it again, God does allow each of us to make choices, for better or for worse. If you are a parent, does He stop you from being mean to your child? Or neglecting your child? Or setting a bad example for your child? Or doing something worse? Then why would you expect Him to stop a pastor from hurting a congregant? And would you conclude that parenting was evil or that families were evil because there are so many bad parents who hurt their children? It's the same with ministry leaders and the church. We cannot conclude that all ministry leaders are evil and that the church is evil because of our own bad experiences or because of some very public scandals.

THERE ARE FAR MORE GOOD APPLES THAN YOU MAY THINK

We all know the saying "one bad apple spoils the barrel," and there is actually truth to this—literal, physiological truth. As one website explained, "One bad, overripe or moldy apple *really* can cause all the other apples around it to spoil. Ethylene gas—a naturally occurring gas that causes fruit to ripen—is to blame."[9] In the same way, one bad person can have a negative effect on his or her colleagues, peers, or fellow leaders.

But that's not the only way the saying is used. It can also mean that one bad apple makes the whole barrel look bad. "If that apple I just grabbed from the barrel is rotten, I don't want to touch the others." Unfortunately, living like this will make us avoid lots and lots of good apples. I know this firsthand, eating two or three apples every day, along with some other fruit. Many times, there's one bad apple in the bag (sometimes two!), but the rest are almost always good, as long as you eat them on time.

In the same way, and this is far more important than apples, for every Christian leader who has fallen, many more have not. It may not feel like that, based on so many recent scandals. And you may have lived through your own spiritual nightmare, where everyone you turned to let you down. But in the spirit of absolute honesty, I must be truthful here as well: Most ministry leaders are not corrupt. Most are not immoral. Most are not in the ministry for selfish material gain or to exert power over others.

To the contrary, the vast majority are in the ministry because they love God and love people. There are far easier jobs, far less stressful jobs, far more lucrative jobs. Most do what they do out of a sense of calling. Even the ones who fall normally start off well but then become corrupt, immoral, or weak along the way, failing to live by biblical principles and guidelines. Let's not throw out all the good because of the bad (as ugly and as inexcusable as that bad has been).

Think about it for a moment. It was tragic to hear about the failings of one of the world's best-known Christian apologists. But he had a whole network of coworkers. How many of them were indicted with similar charges? None to my knowledge.

It's the same with the leaders of Christian colleges and universities. While a Christian university president lost his job over a sex scandal, that was the exception, not the rule. Yes, the leader of one of the largest Christian universities was caught in a serious scandal (although, to be sure, he was never accused of committing adultery or stealing funds). There are hundreds of Christian universities and colleges in America, and it is exceedingly rare to hear about scandals among the senior leaders or even serious charges being brought against them.

In the same way, I do know all too many ministry leaders who have fallen, including a number of the men who served as my pastors or ministry heads during my first twenty years in the Lord. But for each one who fell, I can think of scores of others who did not—people I know personally, people I have worked with closely, people who are full of integrity and with solid marriages, people who are not exploiters or abusers. Why tarnish their solid reputations, earned over decades of faithful service, because of the failings of a small but conspicuous minority?

I once had dinner with Pastor David Wilkerson, sharing with him the devastating news about a pastor I had known for years who had been secretly living in adultery. Him? How could this be? Brother Dave said to me, "For every one who fell, there are three or four who did not."

Honestly, I wanted him to say, "There are three or four hundred who did not" or at least "thirty or forty who did not." But even if his very low estimate was correct, the point remains the same: the ones who sinfully abuse their leadership position are in the minority, often the extreme minority. And even in the midst of human sin and failure, God is still touching lives and bringing about positive change, just as He brought the Savior into the world through the people of Israel, despite the many failings of that nation through the centuries. For a case in point, consider the twelve sons of Jacob, who became the twelve tribes of Israel. They were a dysfunctional mess. Yet God brought redemption to the world through their offspring.

IF YOU PLAY WITH FIRE, YOU WILL BE BURNED

Every single leader who fell, be it sexually or financially or in some other way, did so because they failed to heed biblical warnings. They failed to play by the God-given rules. They ignored the divinely inspired driver's manual. That's how they got off track. Every single one of them. Count on it.

As Proverbs 6:27–29 says, "Can a man scoop fire into his lap without his clothes being burned? Can a man walk on hot coals without his feet being scorched? So is he who sleeps with another man's wife; no one who touches her will go unpunished." And as Paul wrote:

> Do you not know that in a race all the runners run, but only one gets the prize? Run in such a way as to get the prize. Everyone who competes in the games goes into strict training. They do it to get a crown that will not last, but we do it to get a crown that will last forever. Therefore I do not run like someone running aimlessly; I do not fight like a boxer beating the air. No, I strike a blow to my body and make it my slave so that after I have preached to others, I myself will not be disqualified for the prize.
>
> —1 CORINTHIANS 9:24–27

Paul also wrote this to Timothy, a ministry leader and Paul's spiritual son: "Don't let anyone look down on you because you are young, but set an example for the believers in speech, in conduct, in love, in faith and in purity....Be diligent in these matters; give yourself wholly to them, so that everyone may see your progress. Watch your life and doctrine closely. Persevere in them, because if you do, you will save both yourself and your hearers" (1 Tim. 4:12, 15–16). In other words, "Watch yourself, young man!"

For decades now I have warned of the dangers of sexual immorality, recognizing the power of sexual temptation and the frailty of human flesh, my own included, outside of God's empowering help. One of the first points I make when speaking on this, especially when teaching ministry students, is that any of us can fall into sexual sin—and I mean any. If we ignore the traffic signs, we *will* get into an accident. It's as simple and inevitable as that.

If you're a married man and spend too much time with another woman whom you find even slightly attractive, especially time alone (be it in the workplace or via emails or calls or in other private settings), you are opening the door to adultery. And if you refuse to hear the Spirit's correction in your heart or ignore the concerns of others, you will fall even more severely. As the Scripture says, "God resists the proud, but gives grace to the humble" (Jas. 4:6, NKJV).

This leads to an important question: If your doctor gives you explicit post-surgery directives in terms of medications to take and when to go back to work and when to start exercising again and you violate every one of his directives, is it right to blame the doctor when your health fails? If he said, "It is essential you take this pill twice a day without food for the first ten days," and you don't take a single pill, can you be upset with him when you have a relapse? If he said, "Under no circumstances can you lift anything over five pounds or the stitches will tear," and you hit the gym the next day and start bench-pressing two hundred pounds, can you sue him when the wound reopens?

In the same way, God's Word is filled with practical guidelines and strong warnings, especially for leaders, making clear that His standards are high and that He expects His earthly representatives to live by them. Can we blame Him if some of those serving in His name blow it badly and hurt others deeply?

Look at these standards for senior church leadership as laid out by Paul:

> This is a trustworthy saying: "If someone aspires to be a church leader, he desires an honorable position." So a church leader must be a man whose life is above reproach. He must be faithful to his wife. He must exercise self-control, live wisely, and have a good reputation. He must enjoy having guests in his home, and he must be able to teach. He must not be a heavy drinker or be violent. He must be gentle, not quarrelsome, and not love money. He must manage his own family well, having children who respect and obey him. For if a man cannot manage his own household, how can he take care of God's church?
>
> A church leader must not be a new believer, because he might become proud, and the devil would cause him to fall. Also, people outside the church must speak well of him so that he will not be disgraced and fall into the devil's trap.
>
> —1 TIMOTHY 3:1–7, NLT

To the extent that these guidelines are followed by men and women is the extent to which the church will be healthy and believers will be thriving and protected. To the extent that these guidelines are flaunted is the extent to which there will be spiritual sickness and moral corruption, to the harm and hurt of many.

But once again we cannot blame the doctor, as in the Lord, for the failings of those who choose to ignore His directives. Instead, we should recognize that the system He set up is good, one that would protect congregants (the sheep) from abuse, one that would make believers feel safe.

What about all the sexual scandals in the Catholic church? Some of them have been staggering. I am not Catholic, and I have no authority within Catholic circles to make these statements. But I *can* speak as a follower of Jesus, a student of the Word, and an elder in the faith, and an important point needs to be made. The New Testament presupposes that ministry leaders will be married (see the passage just quoted from 1 Timothy 3). Not only so, but Jesus and Paul made clear that only those with the gift of celibacy should remain single. Others do well to marry.[10]

What happens, then, when a system is set up that *requires* priests (or nuns) to be celibate, never marrying for life? Doesn't this open the door to all kinds of temptation and potential abuse? What if you feel called to Catholic ministry and have no desire to marry, not because of holiness but because of homosexuality because you are not attracted to the opposite sex? You now take on celibacy in an environment where you are surrounded by other single men (beginning with seminary), many of whom are also same-sex attracted, and then for decades after that, you're working closely with boys (altar boys). It is any wonder that so many of these boys were abused and so many of these priests fell into sin? And is it any wonder that, over time, a subculture of homosexuality was cultivated in some Catholic leadership circles?

In the words of Cardinal Raymond Burke, "It was clear after the studies following the 2002 sexual abuse crisis that most of the acts of abuse were in fact homosexual acts committed with adolescent young men. There was a studied attempt to either overlook or to deny this. Now it seems clear in light of these recent terrible scandals that indeed there is a homosexual culture, not only among the clergy but even within the hierarchy, which needs to be purified at the root."[11]

Again, a minority of priests and nuns have even been accused of immorality. But that number would be much smaller, in my opinion, had biblical guidelines been followed. That leads me to my final point.

THERE IS A DIFFERENCE BETWEEN WEAKNESS AND WICKEDNESS

Have you ever fallen short? Have you ever disappointed yourself or those you love? Have you had any kind of moral failure, be it sexual or related to character or personal temperament or finances or something else? Have you ever had to say to others, "I'm so sorry! I really let you down"? Or, "I don't know what happened. That is not me. I can't explain why I did this"?

How about before the Lord? How many times have you had to get on your knees or face before Him confessing your sins and your failings: "Lord, I have no excuse, and You don't deserve this! I am so ashamed of myself."

What does our Father do in return? Does He condemn us? Does He cast us away? Does He say, "I don't want to see your face again"? Quite the contrary. He loves us. He comforts us. He consoles us. He forgives us afresh. He gives us hope. He embraces us. And then—this is big—He calls on us to do the same to those who have sinned against us.

As Paul wrote, "Bear with each other and forgive one another if any of you has a grievance against someone. Forgive as the Lord forgave you" (Col. 3:13). Jesus even devoted a whole parable to the subject of forgiving others in the same way He forgave us. He ended it with a very sharp warning for those who refused to forgive.

(See Matthew 18:21–35.) He also warned that we would be judged in the same way that we judged others (Matt. 7:1–5). That's one reason I do my best to extend lots of mercy and compassion to others. The Lord has been incredibly merciful and compassionate to me.

The point is that *all of us* need a Savior. All of us fall short. All of us need mercy. All of us need forgiveness. All of us need God's grace. All of us!

Most ministry leaders who fall are not inherently wicked people. They are often weak people, people who got burned out and lost their sense of propriety. Or they became so consumed with the work of the Lord that they lost their connection to the Lord Himself, opening the door to disaster. Or they thought they could cross a forbidden line just a little, and before they knew it, they could not get back. Then, trapped by the shame of their sin and the fact that coming clean would mean destroying their ministries, hurting the church, devastating their families, and leaving them bereft of income and support, they tried to fix things privately and cover it all up, only making matters worse.

These are often acts of weakness more than wickedness (can you relate to any of this in your own life?), and of the leaders I know who fell, I can think of only one or two who struck me as devious and unrepentant. The others were broken and grieved, recognizing the evil they had done and the trust they had betrayed. Not only so, but ministry leaders are often targets, not just for the devil but for others too. That's why they have to be especially on their guard against opening the door to temptation. Many seducers are out there too.

The point of all this, though, is simple: Jesus can be trusted. Our heavenly Father is faithful. And there are more fine leaders and solid believers than we could meet in a life-time. If you've been hurt by the church, especially by leaders, please don't reject the Lord. He is your best and truest life-line! And then, little by little, reconnect with solid friends who love Him, and get to know some leaders with integrity. You never want to put your total trust in a person the way you trust the Lord, but hopefully in the days and years ahead the good experiences will put the old, painful experiences in the distant past.

For those who feel abandoned or betrayed by God Himself, I encourage you to read my book *Has God Failed You? Finding Faith When You're Not Even Sure God Is Real.*[12]

A FINAL REFLECTION

There's no denying that these scandals have done incalcu-lable damage to those hurt directly, to the reputation of the church, and to the honor of the Lord. They are inexcusable and shameful. But the fact that so much junk has come out in a relatively short period also means that God is acting. He is cleaning house. He is disciplining His children. He is bringing cleansing, repentance, and restoration.

Not only this, but we should not lose sight that a number of major ministries and prominent leaders have been tainted and stained. Could it be that we had our eyes on people? That we overexalted human beings? That we made servants into celebrities? Could it be that the Lord was not pleased with this? (The first time I recall addressing this in writing was in 1989 in my book *The End of the American Gospel Enterprise.*) Could it be that God cut down some of the trees that had grown too high so that He alone could get the glory? Could there be a silver lining in the midst of the pain and disillusionment? I truly believe so.

The Lord often wounds before He heals and brings down before He raises up.[13] May we learn our lessons well.

CHAPTER 4

IF GAY IS GOOD, THE CHURCH IS BAD

AMERICAN CULTURE HAS changed dramatically in the last thirty years. Before that time, Christianity was generally respected by the society while homosexuality was disdained. Today the tables have turned to the point that almost anything LGBTQ+ is celebrated while the church is largely denigrated. In short, if gay is good, the church is bad. This is another reason why many have left the church, especially members of the younger generation.

Consider American views on same-sex "marriage." (For the record, I fully understand that putting "marriage" in quotes marks me as a bigot in the eyes of some of my readers. But I trust that you would prefer I was truthful in my viewpoints rather than hold back just to get you to keep on reading.) A June 1, 2022, Gallup article by Justin McCarthy noted, "When Gallup first polled about same-sex marriage in 1996, barely a quarter of the public (27%) supported legalizing such unions."

The article went on to say that support finally reached the majority level fifteen years later, in 2011, and that four years after that, in 2015, a month before the Supreme Court's *Obergefell v. Hodges* decision, "public support for legalizing gay marriage cracked the 60% level, and last year it reached the 70% mark for the first time." McCarthy reported that as of 2022, support for same-sex "marriage" had reached a high of 71 percent. This is truly remarkable.

Had this poll been conducted in 1986, let alone in 1976 or 1966, support for same-sex "marriage" would have been a fraction of what it is today. But even dating back to 1996, the shift in opinion has been absolutely dramatic, from 27 percent support to 71 percent.

Gallup found that national support for same-sex "marriage" has even risen among people "who have traditionally been the most resistant to gay marriage," and cited as examples those sixty-five and older, who "became mostly supportive in 2016—as did Protestants in 2017 and Republicans in 2021." This reflects changes in public sentiment, with President Obama endorsing these unions in 2012 and the Supreme Court redefining these unions in 2015.

And then the kicker: "Americans who report that they attend church weekly remain the primary demographic holdout against gay marriage, with 40% in favor and 58% opposed." That's why the article had this prominent subheading: "Weekly Churchgoers Are the Final Holdouts of Opposition."[1] We are now the bad guys, the opposition, the ones standing in the way of progress, the small-minded, Bible-thumping bigots, the people who say yes to religion and no to love. That is how much of the world perceives us today, especially the younger generation, which has grown up in a very different world than did previous generations.

LOOKING BACK

In the not-too-distant past, Americans were proud to identify as Christians and ashamed to identify as gays or lesbians. How the tables have turned! Today Christians and Christian beliefs are openly mocked and ridiculed, while day in and day out we hear about gay and lesbian and bi and trans pride, sometimes for weeks on end, almost wherever we turn. As the Catholic conservative Matt Walsh tweeted on March 31, 2022:

> It's a good thing that we have a #TransDayOfVisibility because aside from this day, and Pride Month, and International Pronouns Day, and Lesbian Visibility Day, and International Day Against Homophobia, and Harvey Milk Day, and Pansexual and Panromantic Visibility Day, and (cont)
>
> Bisexuality Day, and Bisexual Awareness Week, and National Coming Out Day, and National LGBT Center Awareness Day, and Spirit Day, and Intersex Awareness Day, and Asexual Awareness Week, and Transgender Day Of Remembrance, and (cont)
>
> Pansexual Pride Day, and Aromantic Spectrum Awareness Week, and Omnisexual Visibility Day, and Non-Binary Awareness Week, and Transgender Parent Day, and every other day and hour and minute of our lives, we really don't celebrate the LGBT community enough.[2]

It wasn't that long ago that the first gay kiss on network TV sparked national controversy. This was in 1991 on *LA*

Law between two women. As a result, NBC reportedly lost some advertisers but then quickly replaced them.[3] And it wasn't until 2000 that there was a "'passionate' kiss between two men on primetime television" (this happened on the show *Dawson's Creek*).[4] Even by 2005, the movie *Brokeback Mountain*, which paints a sympathetic picture of two gay lovers, was considered highly controversial. As explained in a 2015 article:

> *Brokeback Mountain* was released in 2005 and it was a different time—after all, it was 10 years ago. Back then, there were no smartphones and same-sex marriage wasn't even close to being legal. It was a time when a movie like *Brokeback Mountain* would be received in other countries with some controversy.[5]

How times have changed! Today gay and lesbian kisses and other expressions of affection, along with passionate sex scenes, are a dime a dozen on TV, while long-running cable programs have followed the romantic and sexual lives of gays and lesbians.

Back in 1997 controversy abounded when Ellen DeGeneres, playing a TV character named Ellen, came out as lesbian in real life and as the character on the show. Ellen? Really? Today you would be hard-pressed to find a major TV show that doesn't have an LGBTQ+ character, while Ellen herself reigned for years as queen of daytime TV. Even cartoons and children's shows feature LGBTQ+ characters and themes, while the number of gay, bi, or trans superheroes grows every year.[6] Talk about a massive cultural shift. America has never seen anything like it.

I was born in 1955, so for most of my life things were very different than they are today. Still, it's almost hard for me to remember back to when homosexuals hid in the closet and it was illegal for two men (or two women) to dance together in a bar. Today the American Library Association encourages drag queens reading to toddlers, YouTube celebrates little kids in drag, college students start their first classes by giving their names and preferred gender pronouns, and Bruce "Caitlyn" Jenner has been hired as a contributor by "conservative" Fox News.[7] To say it again: America has never seen a cultural shift like this.

And what does it mean for kids who grew up in this new, pro-gay environment? In an April 28, 2017, article titled "How Ellen DeGeneres' Coming Out Changed My Life 20 Years Ago," H. Alan Scott, a gay Jewish comedian, wrote:

> I was 14 when Ellen DeGeneres and her character Ellen Morgan from *Ellen* simultaneously came out as gay on April 30, 1997....But even though it was a groundbreaking moment for TV history, queer people, and society, it was for me the game-changing moment when I knew the walls of the closet I was living in were about to come tumbling down. If what James Baldwin said in *Notes of a Native Son* is correct, that, "People are trapped in history, and history is trapped in them," the moment Ellen DeGeneres uttered the words, "I'm gay," was the moment in my personal history when I knew nothing was ever going to be the same again.[8]

Our grandchildren (born between 2001 and 2006) have grown up in a very different world than my wife and I did (born in 1954 and 1955) or our daughters did (born in 1977 and 1978). They live in a world where they have openly gay or trans classmates (in Christian schools the kids just hide it a little better), a world in which the legalizing of same-sex "marriage" is old news, a world in which President Biden made trans rights one of his major causes, a world in which preschoolers learn about gender identity and queerness.[9] The tide has shifted dramatically.

In the past, being pro-Christian and pro-marriage (meaning, pro-heterosexual marriage) meant swimming with the tide. Today it is the exact opposite. And make no mistake about it: this is an intensely personal issue, not just a theoretical issue. After all, we're talking about someone's child. Or their best friend at school. Or their favorite media personality. "You're telling me that they're going to hell because of who they love? You're telling me they can't serve in your church? If so, I want nothing to do with your religion or your God."

THE SURVEY SAYS...

In *Religion News* on August 6, 2021, Yonat Shimron noted:

> Amid widespread acceptance of LGBTQ people, evangelical church attitudes toward the group have not budged, and the consequences have been dire.
>
> A study last month by the Public Religion Research Institute found the number of Americans who identify as white evangelicals has declined dramatically, from 23% in 2006 to 14.5% in 2020. *Those leaving in the greatest numbers are younger evangelicals whose attitudes toward sexual minorities are starkly at odds with their elders.* Take same-sex marriage: While only one-third (34%) of white evangelicals age 50 and over favor same-sex marriage, 51% of younger white evangelicals ages 18–49 now favor it—a majority, another PRRI study found.[10]

But this is hardly "news" in the sense of something brand-new and surprising. In a February 26, 2014, MSNBC website article, Jane Timm stated:

> *A full 31% of young people (ages 18 to 33) who left orga-nized religion said "negative teachings" or "negative treatment" of gay people was a "somewhat important" or "very important" factor in their departure,* as sur-veyed by the Public Religion Research Institute.
>
> A strong majority (58%) of Americans also said reli-gious groups are "alienating" young people by "being too judgmental on gay and lesbian issues." A full 70% of young people said the same.[11]

And lest you think that this is just a passing fad, consider that according to a controversial 2021 Barna poll, nearly 40 percent of Gen Z young people and 30 percent of Gen Z young Christians describe themselves as being somewhere on the LGBTQ+ spectrum.[12] That is not a typo. Literally four out of ten Gen Z young people in the Barna poll identified as LGBTQ+. A 2021 Gallup poll cuts that number in half but still notes the upsurge in numbers: "Roughly 21% of Generation Z Americans who have reached adulthood—those born between 1997 and 2003—identify as LGBT. That is nearly double the proportion of millennials who do so, while the gap widens even further when compared with older generations."[13]

Even Gallup's lower figures still point to a *dramatic* upturn in LGBTQ+ identification, especially when compared to pre-vious generations:

- Gen Z (born 1997–2003): 20.8%

- Millennials (born 1981–1996): 10.5%

- Gen X (born 1965–1980): 4.2%

- Baby boomers (born 1946–1964): 2.6%

- Traditionalists (born before 1946): 0.8%

It's clear, of course, that only a small percentage of these Gen Z young people are truly same-sex attracted or will struggle long-term with their gender identity. As confirmed in a May 2022 report, "When we look at homosexual behavior, we find that it has grown much less rapidly than LGBT identification. Men and women under 30 who reported a sexual partner in the last five years dropped from around 96% exclusively heterosexual in the 1990s to 92% exclusively heterosexual in 2021. Whereas in 2008 attitudes and behavior were similar, by 2021 LGBT identification was running at twice the rate of LGBT sexual behavior." That's why this report was titled "Born This Way? The Rise of LGBT as a Social and Political Identity."[14]

Put another way, for some young people, identifying as bi or trans is a statement of solidarity with their LGBTQ+ friends. Or is it an expression of their desire to appear "open" or "tolerant" or "woke"? Or is it a way to challenge the status quo or rebel against the older generation? (In my day the guys grew their hair long, the girls became more promiscuous, and we all got high together.) Either way, with so many identifying as somewhere on the queer spectrum, they now set themselves against biblical values—and they perceive *us* as being against *them*. This is a real issue for the gospel and a problem we must address. And to the extent that, as Christians, we have become better known for being anti-gay than pro-Jesus, the problem is much worse.

Americans like to root for the underdog, and today many young people feel solidarity with people who are marginalized, who appear to be the victims. This is especially true when the marginalized are their friends and family members. "When you reject them, you reject me!" That's why so many Americans, especially young people, feel great solidarity with those who identify as LGBTQ+.

Not only this, but some of these young people grew up hearing about the evils of homosexuality, as if all gays and lesbians were the worst of sinners and the most vile of moral monsters and as if same-sex couples couldn't really love each other or the kids they were raising. Yet as they grew older, they met nice, considerate coworkers who were gay, and gay couples who were just like their parents (other than being the same sex), and kids raised by gay parents who were well-adjusted and successful.

Where does that leave Christians who teach that homosexual practice is sinful and that God made us either male or female? We are viewed as mean-spirited, narrow-minded, hateful, and judgmental. Little wonder so many choose their friends over their faith, especially when that faith is so caricatured and misunderstood.

In his 2019 book, *Resilient Faith: How the Early Christian "Third Way" Changed the World*, professor Gerald Sittser states plainly, "The fact is: Christianity in America is declining, in both numbers and influence. The culture is changing, and we must therefore recognize that we live in a world very different from the one that existed even half a century ago during what appeared to be the 'golden age' of American Christianity."

He continues, "You probably sense the change and observe the trends, too. You know about the decline of mainline churches; the lack of growth in evangelical churches; the rise of 'dones' (Christian dropouts) and 'nones' (those people who refuse to identify with any religious tradition)...the creeping loss of religious freedom; the growing dominance of secularity in the public square; the deterioration of traditional morality in the entertainment industry."[15]

Exactly so. And nowhere can this be seen more clearly than in the mercurial rise and thunderous celebration of everything LGBTQ+. The consequences for the church have been disastrous.

In the late 1960s, when gay activists came to national attention and began to organize together, they realized that the two main obstacles standing in their path were the world of psychology and the world of religion. Psychology looked at homosexuality as something aberrant, something wrong. Religion looked at homosexuality as something sinful. That's why, for many years, a "gay Christian" mantra has been, "Not a sin, not a sickness."

The first obstacle was quickly overcome when, in the 1970s, both APAs (the American Psychological Association and the American Psychiatric Association) depathologized homosexuality, no longer treating it as a disorder. The second obstacle, the battle with the conservative church of America, rages on to this day.

How is this battle being won by LGBTQ+ activists and their allies? It is not on the theological front, where churches and denominations that change their teaching continue to lose members. It is not by using the Bible to promote homosexuality and transgenderism, since that remains a losing battle.[16] Rather, it is by human empathy and by popularity. In the words of a mother, spoken with tears on a viral video, "I was being asked to choose [between] my child and my church. I chose my child."[17]

Surveying the religious landscape of Europe, *The Guardian* noted in 2019 that "Europe's march towards a post-Christian society has been starkly illustrated by research showing a majority of young people in a dozen countries do not follow a religion." More specifically, "The survey of 16- to 29-year-olds found the Czech Republic is the least religious country in Europe, with 91% of that age group saying they have no religious affiliation. Between 70% and 80% of young adults in Estonia, Sweden and the Netherlands also categorise themselves as non-religious."

The article also pointed out that in the UK "70 percent of young people identify with no religion" and 59 percent "never attend religious services." In the words of theology and religion professor Stephen Bullivant, "Christianity as a default, as a norm, is gone, and probably gone for good—or at least for the next 100 years."[18] (I would add that this would be true barring a fresh wave of revival; it is not a *fait accompli*.)

At the same time (no coincidence!), an LGBT+ Pride 2021 Global Survey by Ipsos pointed to "a wide generation gap around gender identity and sexual attraction." Specifically, "On average, across the 27 countries surveyed" 4 percent of Generation Z "identify as transgender, non-binary, non-conforming, gender-fluid, or other than male or female" while the same can be said for just 1 percent of all adults. "Younger adults are also significantly more likely to identify differently from heterosexual and to say they are equally attracted to both sexes."[19]

So while these numbers represent much lower percentages than in America, where there has been a massive spike in LGBTQ+ identification among young people, the pattern is the same. The younger you are, the more likely you are to identify as LGBTQ+ and the more likely you are to be irreligious.

BUT THERE'S MORE TO THE STORY THAN MEETS THE EYE

At this point, if you consider yourself a Bible-believing Christian, you might say, "Then what do we do? We can't compromise or change what the Bible says. But we don't want to push people away from the Lord. Help!"

Well, I have some encouragement for you. First, the gospel is still good news—and that means for everyone, however "queer" they may be. Jesus alone forgives, delivers, transforms, and liberates, and life in Him cannot possibly be compared to life outside of Him. That's why another tide is rising in our midst, namely, the ex-gay, ex-trans tide, the tide of men and women who are finding new life in Jesus. Their voices cannot be silenced forever![20]

Second, as we have predicted for years, LGBTQ+ activists continue to overplay their hand, while the trajectory of LGBTQ+ ideals, values, and lifestyles continues to become more extreme. That's one reason I use all these initials along with the plus sign. It's a reminder that once you deviate from the God-ordained norms, there is no limit to how far you can go.

That's also why there is an increasing pushback against LGBTQ+ activism, as many Americans who changed their views on same-sex relationships ("Who are we to say no to love?") did not sign up for boys who identify as girls sharing locker rooms with their daughters or playing on the same sports teams.

And not just the older generation is having second thoughts. As a headline and subhead on a 2019 Jonathan Van Maren blog noted, "Young people pushing back against transgender nonsense has LGBT activists alarmed. Young people simply do not believe that women can have penises, that men can get pregnant, or that gender is fluid."[21]

They did not sign up for drag queens reading to their toddlers in libraries. Or for tampons to be put in men's bathrooms on college campuses since "men menstruate too." Or for a national debate to be triggered over the question "What is a woman?" Or for Disney films pushing more and more LGBTQ+ characters in their children's movies. They certainly didn't sign up for major companies, including Burger King, Dr. Pepper, and Postmates (which is owned by Uber), airing ads during "Pride Month" in June celebrating aspects of *anal sex*.[22] (I'm not making this up.)

But this is the inevitable trajectory of LGBTQ+ activism, as I predicted in detail in 2011 in *A Queer Thing Happened to America*. The handwriting was on the wall for all to see, and the biblical principle that everything reproduces after its own kind made clear in which direction this activism would go. So while it is true that the vast majority of Americans favor laws protecting LGBTQ+ individuals,[23] the trajectory of queer activism will eventually erode that support. To cite Van Maren again:

> According to the annual Accelerating Acceptance report, the number of Americans between the ages of 18 and 34 who are "comfortable interacting with LGBTQ people" dropped from 53% in 2017 to 45% in 2018, which is already a decrease from 63% in 2016....This is the only age group that is growing more uncomfortable with the LGBTQ movement—and this is the famously "tolerant" generation. Young women in particular are driving this

change, with their comfort levels dropping from 64% in 2017 to 52% in 2018 according to a recent Harris Poll commissioned by the gay activist organization GLAAD.[24]

Van Maren goes on to say that youth "have a front-row seat to the chaos the LGBTQ movement is wreaking on their schools," and that teenage girls "are suing their schools over bathroom privacy and biological males in female sports competitions. Their childhoods are being turned into battlefields in the culture wars, and many of them are profoundly unhappy with this."[25]

I wrote in July 2021:

> I recently explained that, as much as I am sympathetic to the goals of gay Americans who feel that they are simply fighting for equality and freedom, I cannot support those goals for two reasons. The first is biblical: same-sex relationships and endless gender variations violate God's best plan for humanity. The second is social: when we look at the trajectory of LGBTQ+ activism, we see that it ends up going in a very dangerous and destructive direction.
>
> Recently, a man who identifies as a woman shocked patrons at a local spa when he exposed himself to the women and girls there. This led to protests condemning his behavior as well as defending his "rights," with one protest turning violent thanks to the presence of Antifa.
>
> To be sure, there were many in the LGBTQ+ community who were appalled, saying this is *not* what they stand for.
>
> As reported on Fox News, Tammy Bruce "a member of the LGBTQ community herself, told Tucker Carlson

on Monday that the exchange was troubling to many of her 'transgender friends' who found the individual's behavior offensive.

"'My concern here is that the average transgender person, and I have perhaps more transgender friends than some of the people watching the program, they are also appalled,' Bruce said."

So, the trajectory of which I am speaking is *not* that there will suddenly be an epidemic of biological males who claim to be females exposing themselves to women and girls. (Sadly, this *has* happened in the past, and it's another reason why biological males should not have access to women's bathrooms and locker rooms and the like.)

The trajectory of which I speak is the trajectory of social madness, resulting in headlines like this, from the *Daily Mail*: "Violent clashes break out in LA between rival protesters after viral video showed customer complaining about transgender woman exposing their penis to children in upmarket spa's steam room."

Just look at this four-word phrase: "woman exposing their penis" (and yes, *never forget* that he did this in the presence of girls). What kind of madness is this?[26]

And what about the growing number of young people who are detransitioning, meaning trying to reverse their sex-change surgeries and the effects of their hormone treatments? How long will their voices be ignored? How many more horror stories will we need to hear?[27] How many more times do we need to read about a nineteen-year-old girl who now accepts herself as a girl but who already had a full mastectomy?

No wonder that a mother (herself a political liberal in favor of same-sex "marriage") called this push to transition kids the "largest medical scandal in history."[28] No wonder that there are now more than *thirty-five thousand* members of a Reddit detransitioning group.[29] The mother of an eighteen-year-old girl who suddenly began identifying as a boy wrote to me after visiting this Reddit group, saying, "You have probably had more detransition stories than you want to know about, but I just discovered Reddit dtrans. 35,000 members, mostly people detransitioned and their stories. It is absolutely tearing me up, I'm crying and am so angry that people even are pushing for this! I'm so distressed!"

She continued, "This is why I'm crying. Most people said they were questioning as kids 12–14. Then went on social media and found the cool people who transitioned or society told them it was the best thing for their dysphoria. Now they have woken up and are devastated. Like Scott Newgent said, most suicides are 7–10 years after transitioning when people say what on earth did I do to myself!"[30] (Scott Newgent, whom I know as Kellie and who has become a friend, is a "trans man" (meaning, a female to male) who is now shouting at the top of her lungs, warning against transitioning children and making clear that no amount of surgery or hormones can make her into a man.)[31]

Or listen to the story of Keira Bell, a young woman in England who, after she "kept insisting that I wanted to be a boy," was referred to a gender identity clinic and, at age sixteen, put on puberty blockers. One year later, she was receiving testosterone shots. Then, at twenty and sporting a beard, she had a double mastectomy, living her life as Quincy.

Sometime later, she realized that she was neither Quincy nor a male. Instead, she had other emotional and psychological issues. But in these days of transanity, she was completely misdiagnosed. Where did all this leave her?

"The consequences of what happened to me," she explains, "have been profound: possible infertility, loss of my breasts and inability to breastfeed, atrophied genitals, a permanently changed voice, facial hair. When I was seen at the Tavistock clinic, I had so many issues that it was comforting to think I really had only one that needed solving: I was a male in a female body. But it was the job of the professionals to consider all my co-morbidities, not just to affirm my naïve hope that everything could be solved with hormones and surgery."[32]

All is not as it appears to be—or as the media and social media often portray things. Perhaps there are painful consequences from deviating from God's male-female order? Perhaps our Maker knew what He was doing?

Consider that in a Center for the Study of Partisanship and Ideology report, Eric Kauffman, a University of London political scientist and professor, noted: "Very liberal ideology and LGBT identification are associated with anxiety and depression in young people. Very liberal young Americans are twice as likely as others to experience these problems. 27% of young Americans with anxiety or depression were LGBT in 2021. This relationship appears to have strengthened since 2010."[33]

So even with increased acceptance of LGBTQ+ people and identities, they still struggle in these areas. Specifically, according to the website Calm Sage, a "community working towards changing the way individuals think & act about problems related to Mental Health":

- The link between homosexuality and depression is six times more prevalent than for heterosexual counterparts.

- The suicide rate among the LGBTQ+ community is three times higher than the heterosexual suicide rate.

- Around 20–30% of LGBTQ+ people abuse substances, and the major reasons behind this are gay depression, lesbian depression, gay anxiety, and LGBTQ+ prejudices.

- On average 30–60% of lesbians, bisexuals, transgender people, or gay men deal with depression and anxiety.[34]

To be clear, the website posting these statistics claims that more acceptance of those who identify as LGBTQ+ is a major factor in their emotional wholeness and that "the majority of LGBTQIA++ community members lead happy, healthy, and fulfilling lives with their partners."[35] Still, we can only wonder: if God indeed made us male and female as a reflection of His image, and if He intended marriage to be exclusively male-female, both for the sake of the couples and their children, then deviating from this plan will have dire consequences. Little surprise, then, that teachers in pre-K talk to their three- and four-year-old students about being nonbinary and queer, that kids in kindergarten are encouraged to look for their trans identity, and that J. K. Rowling (author of the Harry Potter books) gets attacked and threatened for saying only women menstruate.

In fact, the attempts to cancel Rowling and others (who are liberal in their ideology and morals) for daring to challenge any aspect of LGBTQ+ activism means that the tables have turned—now the LGBTQ+ community has become the big bully, and people who dissent (especially Christian conservatives) are being bullied. As I've been saying since 2014, those who came out of the closet now want to put us in the closet. Perhaps this will cause a change in public sentiment too?[36]

The problem for true followers of Jesus is that the Bible hasn't changed, which means that God is still against homosexual practice and identity. So if we want to be in solidarity with the Lord, we will find ourselves at odds with the prevailing culture. At the same time, we do not want to drive people away from the Lord by making opposition to LGBTQ+ activism our primary cause (as opposed to being disciples and making disciples being our primary cause). Nor do we ever want to appear (or be) mean-spirited, judgmental, or hypocritical. What, then, do we do?

First, we ask God to fill our hearts with His love for those who identify as LGBTQ+, and we seek to share that love with them face to face. Second, we make clear in our messages that all of us are fundamentally flawed, which is why all of us need a Redeemer. Third, we make a distinction between an aggressive agenda and individual people. Fourth, we determine to hold to biblical standards regardless of public opinion (and regardless of how much these standards challenge our own lives). Fifth, we give ourselves to prayer, also believing that those with antibiblical values will continue to overplay their hand, further exposing the wrongness of their position. Sixth, we share the testimonies of those who have been transformed through the gospel, making clear that our message is filled with hope and life. Seventh, we let the chips fall where they may, determined to preach Jesus and live for Jesus no matter what, always remembering that this world is not our eternal home.

It is true that for many reasons people are leaving the church over LGBTQ+ issues and concerns. It is also true that many others are meeting Jesus powerfully. That's because what the world so desperately needs we have in the fullness of the gospel. Let us not be ashamed to live it and proclaim it.

MAY I HAVE ONE MORE WORD WITH YOU?

If you differ with my position and still feel justified in leaving the church and rejecting the Bible, please ask yourself these questions: First, can you at least see that it is love that motivates us to speak up and reach out? We're not trying to control people's lives. We simply believe that God's design is best. Second, are you sure that things in the LGBTQ+ community are on a healthy trajectory? New gender identities and preferred gender pronouns, which are virtually endless, are leading us to who knows where. Transgender activism has now come to the point of mutilating healthy body parts and sterilizing healthy young people, in many cases irreversibly. Can you see now why we have raised our voices?

Third, is it really so bigoted to think that kids do best with a mom and a dad? That there's a reason that *every human being* that comes into the world is the product of a male and female, without exception. (Obviously, we're not talking about Adam, Eve, and Jesus!) That the world's best dad is not a mom and the world's best mom is not a dad, and that two dads or two moms, however loving they may be, cannot equal a mom and a dad, each of whom are wired differently and provide unique contributions to a child's upbringing, as confirmed by countless studies? Is it hate that moves us to say these things or love?

Remember that it is our voices—the voices of Bible-believing Christians—that are being shut down and canceled. Our YouTube channels, Facebook pages, and Instagram accounts are being removed simply because we teach what the Bible says. Do you feel good about attempts to silence *us*? Is that the way of tolerance, inclusion, and diversity? And if what we're saying can be so easily refuted, why are people so afraid to let us speak? Could it be that our words are like light shining in darkness and that some people are trying to silence us because we're speaking the truth? Could it be?

Please do give this some thought.

CHAPTER 5

THE POLITICIZING
OF THE GOSPEL

IT'S ONE THING for Christians to be involved politically, to vote for their preferred candidates and advocate for issues that are important to them. It's another thing to make politics a central part of our faith. Or to divide over political allegiance. Or to become so associated with a particular candidate or party that we become better known as followers of that candidate—or members of that party—than we are known as followers of Jesus. When we do this, we cheapen the gospel and add another requirement to the faith: "You must believe in Jesus and embrace our particular political position. Otherwise, you're not welcome here." We may not say it quite like that, but that's the overall effect.

In the 2020 elections, it seemed as if we heard more about Trump in our church circles—for him or against him—than we heard about Jesus. It seemed as if our social media pages were dominated by political debate, much of it quite passionate, with the Bible weaponized to support our position and bash our opponents. Even our tone changed, as we became just like the world: angry, judgmental, spiteful, mocking, divided, and divisive.

Where was the Spirit of God in all this? What happened to the words of Jesus, that the world would know we were His disciples because of our love for one another? (See John 13:34–35.) Things got so bad that I actually wrote an article titled "And They Will Know We Are Christians by Our Hate."[1]

No wonder many people walked out of the church over this. No wonder many were offended. No wonder many thought, "I come here to worship God and grow in the Word and enjoy fellowship with my brothers and sisters. Instead, what I experienced in church today felt more like a political rally."

I voted for Donald Trump in 2016 and 2020 because of his pro-life, pro-religion, pro-Israel positions (among others), believing that he was better for America (and frankly for world stability) than Hillary Clinton or Joe Biden. At the same time, I realized how abrasive he could be, how mean-spirited, narcissistic, carnal, and reckless. And I realized that because he had become such a good friend of evangelical Christians—to this day, that remains the case—we were now widely associated with Trump, especially White evangelicals. Trump was our man!

That's why I kept shouting from the rooftops, "Jesus is my Savior. He gets my heart and soul, my lifelong devotion, my blood. Trump is my president. He gets my vote." That's why, as a Trump voter, I wrote a book in 2018 titled *Donald Trump Is Not My Savior: An Evangelical Leader Speaks His Mind About the Man He Supports as President.*[2] I followed this up in 2020 with *Evangelicals at the Crossroads: Will We*

Pass the Trump Test?[3] By the "Trump test" I meant: 1) Can we vote for Trump without compromising our witness? and 2) Can we unite around Jesus even if we differ over Trump? I don't think we passed the test. Instead, we failed badly.

Yet despite writing these books and making these statements, I too had to fight off the political fever, the feeling of being consumed day and night with the elections, the sense that the fate of the nation was hanging on the outcome of the vote. I'm also sure that some Christians (and non-Christians) saw me as an apologist for Trump as well. I know it because I heard from them on a regular basis.

In some of our circles, loyalty to the Lord was judged by our loyalty to or rejection of Trump. He, rather than Jesus, became the dividing line. How on earth did this happen? Some Trump supporters even made him into a bigger-than-life figure. *Only Trump can save America. Only Trump can be trusted. Only Trump will fight for us. God has specially anointed Donald Trump for such a time as this!*

Personally, I am deeply grateful to President Trump for the good things that he did and the promises he kept. In many ways the list of his accomplishments is exceptional and in some ways unprecedented. I will mention some of them in this chapter. On a certain level, I believe he was raised up by God in a unique and powerful way.

At the same time, he left a wake of destruction in his path, the worst of which was felt in the church. That's because in many ways we became like him, emulating his worst qualities, dividing with our own brothers and sisters (God calls us to unity!), and putting him on such a high pedestal that it bordered on idolatry. Not only did this offend the Lord, but it offended many people, both Christian and non-Christian.

I'm aware, of course, that the Left-leaning media savaged Trump, treating him unfairly and even lying about him at times. And I'm aware that because of his extraordinary backbone, he was hated all the more for his stands. So the critics added to the anti-Trump sentiments, making those who supported him look even worse. We—especially those of us who are White—were branded White supremacists and insurrectionists. This, in turn, drummed up more hatred toward us and, from our side, more solidarity with Trump, since we saw that we were now being lied about and misrepresented, just as he was.

But to the extent that we became known as vocal, passionate, *Christian* supporters and defenders of Trump, the gospel now became mixed with politics and Jesus became mixed with a very flawed man. What a dangerous—even fatal—mistake.

It's one thing to be apologists for the Lord. He is perfect and beautiful and glorious, without blemish or flaw or imperfection. It is another thing to be apologists for flawed, fallen human beings. They are anything but perfect, beautiful, glorious, without blemish or flaw or imperfection. It's one thing to preach Jesus. It's another thing to preach Trump (or Obama or Hillary or Biden). What a putrid mixing of the Spirit with the flesh!

The difference between our devotion to Jesus and our devotion to any political leader should be the difference between heaven and earth. The world should hear us *shouting* our love for the Lord and our loyalty to Him, in word and in deed. Our preferred candidate gets our vote. Instead, we were shouting our loyalty to a candidate. You can be assured that the world took notice.

We also have to remember that we were known as the

values voters, the ones who proclaimed, "Character counts! Morality matters!" We were the ones who were outraged over Bill Clinton's sexual failures. "A man like that should not be leading our country!" Now we were enthusiastically supporting Trump? Now we were vying for photo-ops with a thrice-married former playboy who made millions of dollars on casinos, some of them housing strip clubs as well? Evangelicals and Donald Trump? *Are you kidding me?*

Some would say, "But you're comparing apples with oranges. Trump did those things before we embraced him as our candidate. Bill Clinton committed his sins in the White House."

That, of course, is true (although Clinton was accused of sexual assault long before he was president). But did we support Trump any less when the infamous *Access Hollywood* tapes were released, exposing some of his most vulgar comments about women?[4]

Some might say, "Those words were inexcusable. But he did apologize for them, and Melania made clear that that is not the man he is today. Again, that's who he was in the past."

Fair enough. But if similar tapes exposed a Democratic presidential candidate, would we have let him or her off the hook so easily? Would we not have shouted, "We could never vote for someone like that!"? And weren't we the same ones who believed President Clinton's many sexual accusers but dismissed the women who accused Trump of sexual assault or harassment? Do we really think the world wasn't watching? Were we following the biblical principle of equal weights and measures, or were we engaging in partisan political ethics?

YES, PEOPLE DID LEAVE THE
CHURCH OVER THIS

I heard this story firsthand from a pastor of a thriving congregation in a major American city. In fact, after he shared this with some leaders in a conference call, I interviewed him personally to be sure I had the details right.

About fifteen hundred people were in his church, with a large percentage of them millennials. In keeping with the ethnic makeup of their location, the congregation was largely White and Asian. While the church had a great heart for worship and encountering the Spirit of God, it was also concerned about social issues to the point that it had a "Justice Department."

But things began to unravel in 2016 when White evangelicals became so identified with Donald Trump, making many of the congregants uneasy. Would they now be viewed as being staunch Trump supporters as well? Then, when the *Access Hollywood* tape was released, many in the church were repulsed, especially when evangelical leaders seemed to minimize the ugliness of Trump's words. At this point, some of these congregants got up and left, especially the younger ones.

When George Floyd was killed and things became divided between "us" and "them"—with "them" being the White supremacists and Trump supporters—an uproar broke out, *with every single member of the Justice Department resigning and leaving the church.* In the end, as much as 20 percent of the congregation left over issues related to Donald Trump and race. This is how volatile things became.

At the same time, many sincere believers had become

so concerned with the direction the nation was going—for good reason—that we merged patriotism with the gospel. (As some have put it, we wrapped the gospel in the American flag.) "America is a Christian nation, and Trump is our defender. He is the man raised up by God to stop this dangerous slide to the Left!" And so not only did we preach both Jesus and Trump together (obviously, not in the same way, but in a connected way; just look at the prayer, worship, and preaching that took place at his rallies), but we also merged the cross and flag. They now became totally intertwined.

To make a candid confession, I endorsed Senator Ted Cruz for president in 2016, speaking a couple of times at his rallies in North Carolina. And I did use the platform to preach Jesus, call us to repentance, and speak of the need for a gospel-based moral and cultural revolution. But I also made some political comments (at that time, during the primaries, for Cruz and against Trump, although not by name), something I had never done in my entire life. (Before this I had never endorsed a candidate. I do not plan to endorse a candidate again.) At a weeklong prayer retreat in late 2020, I listened to one of those messages, which was about four minutes long, and I wept before the Lord as I listened. I had mixed politics with the gospel in an unhealthy way, preaching Jesus one moment and taking aim (in a lighthearted way) at another political candidate. I had become partisan.

AMERICA NEEDS JESUS BECAUSE AMERICANS NEED JESUS

The reality is that America, like every other nation on the planet, is part of the fallen world system. Believers in

America, along with believers in every country, make up the *ekklesia*, the church or Messianic congregation. But America itself, speaking of the entire nation, is filled with sin and guilt, including the blood of the slaughtered unborn; all kinds of sexual immorality and perversion; greed and decadence and addiction; and day-and-night violence. We are hardly a "Christian nation" despite the vast majority of Americans professing to be Christian. In truth, only a remnant is truly devoted to the Lord.

Yet somehow "Make America Great Again" became part of our spiritual mantra (rather than "Your Kingdom Come to America") to the point that we could more easily be identified by our MAGA hats than by our Christlike behavior. Added to this was the large chorus of prophets announcing Trump's reelection and guaranteeing him four more years in the White House. Surely these men and women of God could not be wrong!

And what happened if you dared to differ with the narrative, even as a Trump voter? What happened if you dared question "the prophets"? What happened if you called for accountability? What happened if you appealed for decent, respectful interaction? What happened if you raised a concern that we were looking to Trump in an unhealthy, even idolatrous way? You were savaged by Christ followers. You were brutalized. You were accused of being weak and spineless. Your loyalty to Jesus was questioned (seriously!). You were accused of being a liberal and a leftist and a Communist and a baby killer (really!). Talk about an almost cultlike devotion to Trump. It was heartbreaking to behold. (For details, including actual quotes, see my book *The Political Seduction of the Church*.)

No wonder so many believers got turned off and walked out. No wonder so many non-Christians shook their heads and said, "I knew it was always a matter of power and control. That's all the religious Right ever cared about." No wonder the name of the Lord and the reputation of the church took such a bad hit. We dragged Jesus down into our political divisions rather than proclaiming Him as Lord, standing totally above the political fray.

As Pastor Andy Stanley wrote in his book *Not in It to Win It*:

> If you attend or pastor a predominantly white church where demonizing the Democratic Party or party leaders by name is commonplace and applauded, you should put a sign in the lobby that reads, We are unapologetically pro-Republican. Why not?...
>
> And in keeping with my goal of being an equal opportunity offender, if you attend or pastor a predominantly Black or Brown church that is unapologetically political, you should put up a sign as well. Why not? Seriously, why not? "That's ridiculous, Andy" is not a reason.
>
> Why not let people know that, in addition to the gospel, your church has a political agenda. Let 'em know that if their political views don't line up with the political views of the leadership of the church, they will never feel at home in your church. Why not?[5]

WHAT ABOUT THE CULTURE WARS?

You might say: "I totally agree with you on this. The church got way too involved politically. And we definitely divided over Trump, for him and against him. We didn't handle the moment well. But what are we to do about our nation? Our precious religious freedoms were under attack—freedoms we want to pass on to our children and grandchildren—and God used Trump to fight for those. The blood of the unborn was screaming from the ground—and God used Trump to appoint the justices who overturned *Roe v. Wade*. Trump also moved our embassy to Jerusalem, brokered the Abraham Accords, canceled our disastrous nuclear treaty with Iran, stood up to Communist China, and faced down North Korea. In short, his presidency might have saved millions of lives. Do we just do nothing today, waiting for our heavenly home tomorrow? Do we not get involved here on earth at all?"

Of course we get involved here on earth. That is the gospel too. After all, the Great Commission is go and make disciples, and disciples are called to be the salt of the earth and the light of the world. (See Matthew 5:13–16; 28:18–20.) Of course we stand for justice and righteousness. Of course we help the poor and the oppressed. Of course we unite against international terrorism and oppression. And though some might disagree with me, we also fight for the lives of the unborn and push back against unhealthy LGBTQ+ activism. As we do so, we will be hated and reviled and rejected. So be it. That comes with the territory.

But it's one thing to be hated for your pro-life stand. It's another thing to be hated for your vocal political affiliation. It's one thing to be reviled for standing for marriage as God intended it. It's another to be reviled for affirming false prophetic words. It's one thing to be rejected for speaking the truth in love. It's another thing to be rejected for acting like jerks. Politics is often dirty and ugly and corrupt. Jesus is spotless and beautiful and pure. The two do not mix well.

In recent years it has become common on our social media pages to see Bible memes side by side with political attack memes. One minute a believer is posting a beautiful verse from the Bible extolling the mercy and kindness of the Lord. Next is a link to a glorious worship song that takes you right into God's presence. Then there's a meme featuring the picture of a political candidate we do not like (should I say we despise?) accompanied by some mocking, demeaning quote. How can this be? As Jacob (James)[6] wrote, "With the tongue we praise our Lord and Father, and with it we curse human beings, who have been made in God's likeness. Out of the same mouth come praise and cursing. My brothers and sisters, this should not be. Can both fresh water and salt water flow from the same spring? My brothers and sisters, can a fig tree bear olives, or a grapevine bear figs? Neither can a salt spring produce fresh water" (Jas. 3:9–12). Doesn't this sound as if he wrote this for us today? Doesn't it sound like he was reading some of our posts and comments?

I do not see how mocking President Biden's mental facilities (if you're a Republican) or mocking President Trump's weight (if you're a Democrat) has anything to do with Jesus. Or the gospel. Or the Holy Spirit. Or the Bible. Nor do I see how repeating the latest inflammatory political headline (without even investigating what is written) comports with the spirit of truth.

Referring to Christian leaders who sounded no different than the latest political attack ad, Pastor Stanley wrote, "They taught their children to behave better. Their children should have taken their phones away. They betrayed their Savior, and they abused their influence. Even worse, their irresponsible, adolescent behavior empowered their followers and their congregants to follow suit."[7]

We really should be ashamed of ourselves—not all of us, for sure. But if the shoe fits, let's wear it. Even if we didn't fall into this type of carnal behavior, we can't deny that our very public, very open, very aggressive political stances—often filled with flesh and carnality—drove people from Jesus.

If you are one of those who walked away because of this, I don't blame you. Just as you don't go to a quiet restaurant to be lectured about politics or to a ballgame to watch political commercials, you certainly don't go to church to hear one candidate exalted and another candidate bashed. You go there to hear about Jesus.

How, then, do we move forward? How do we reach those who have become offended? How do we bring them back? Let me answer those questions by speaking directly to those who left church or lost faith or wrote off Christians because of the politicizing of the gospel.

CAN I SHARE SOME THOUGHTS WITH YOU?

If you find yourself in agreement with my assessment, saying, "That's exactly why I left the church," then can I ask you some honest questions? Did you actually attend a church service where you heard the pastor extolling a political candidate or party rather than preaching Jesus? Did you hear sermons in your home congregation when your pastor used the Bible as a political weapon rather than as a life-transforming, holy book? If so, you experienced the exception to the rule, and I'm terribly sorry for it. But from everything I know, based on my extensive interaction with pastors and national leaders, the vast majority of churches in America did not depart from their normal preaching and teaching during the election seasons. The vast majority of pastors did not focus on politics during those turbulent times.

"But," you say, "I thought you agreed with me that many of

the churches *did* engage in overt partisan politics? Now I'm confused."

To explain, I was speaking primarily of the behavior of lots of individual Christians on their social media pages and in their personal interactions as opposed to what most pastors and leaders were saying from their pulpits. When it came to Christian leaders, a number of prominent evangelicals became outspoken supporters of Trump—champions for Trump, really—seen with him at political rallies or stumping for him on major news channels. This, then, gave the feeling that the evangelical church as a whole was in bed with Donald Trump politically, that we had sold our souls for a seat at the table, that we had exchanged our spiritual influence for national power. (I'm not saying these accusations were all true; I'm saying that this was the perception of many, understandably so.) Making things even worse were the "Trump prophets," now invoking the name of God for their always-affirming, totally partisan, pro-Trump words. (I devoted two lengthy chapters to this subject in *The Political Seduction of the Church*.)

Once again, the few made the many look bad. The handful of heavily political apples gave the impression that the whole barrel of apples was deeply partisan. Maybe it wasn't your pastor on TV making the pro-Trump arguments and quoting verses to support the president, but it sure felt like it.

The fact is, with rare exception, if you had walked into most evangelical churches during the 2020 or 2022 election seasons, you would have experienced church as normal. There would have been worship (of Jesus, not the president). There would have been announcements and an offering.

There would have been a time for prayer. And there would have been a Bible-based, practical message.

There *might* have been a word of encouragement to remember to pray for the elections. There *might* have been voter guides available in the foyer, letting you know where candidates stood on each major issue (just for your information, without endorsing a particular candidate). But in most churches you would not have found these useful tools (what's wrong with being informed?). And in most churches not a word would have been said about politics.

Is it possible that you overreacted, judging your pastor or local church by others' behavior? Did you throw out the baby with the bathwater? I've certainly done that at times, making a hasty decision or judging the whole by the part. Is it possible you did the same?

You might reply, "But that's the issue. It wasn't just the part. Maybe my pastor didn't get overtly political, but the congregants sure did. Maybe the church service seemed pretty normal, but our conversations over meals didn't sound the same, and our social media feeds were horrible. It was politics, politics, politics, day and night. And be assured that you were judged harshly if you dared to deviate even the slightest bit from the standard talking points."

To this I say, "Guilty as charged!" That's exactly what happened in far too many of our circles. We *did* get consumed. We *did* get caught up. We *did* get in the flesh. You are absolutely right, and that's a large reason why I wrote *Evangelicals at the Crossroads* along with *The Political Seduction of the Church*. We really did disgrace ourselves in many unseemly ways.

For this I say to you (as a church leader and a member of

the body): Please forgive us. We fell short. We dishonored the Lord. We disrespected you. We blew it, and you got hurt as a result. But please do not write us off (or, even more, the Lord) forever. We do care about your well-being. We do want to see you blessed and thriving in the Lord. And we really do love our communities. We just got caught up in the political spirit because we were so passionate about the issues, about very important issues. Still, we crossed some dangerous lines. We own our mistake, and we pledge to learn from it and move forward.

PERHAPS THIS WILL HELP

Having said all that from the heart, without qualification or justification, please allow me to explain just how this all came down. Perhaps if you can see things through our eyes it might help you understand why so many good and godly people got so carnal. (Again, this is not an excuse or justification. It is an explanation.)

Let's say we lived in the days of slavery in America, somewhere in the 1850s. Opposition to this foul institution was reaching a fever pitch in certain parts of our nation, while in other parts slavery was a way of life. Mess with the system, and you mess with us. One political candidate and party stood firmly against slavery, pledging to abolish it. The other candidate and party passionately defended slavery, threatening to secede from the union.

Do you really think that if you and I were alive at that time we would have separated politics from the gospel? To the contrary, we would have joined them together, arguing that a true Christian was duty bound and love bound to fight against slavery. How could you be a follower of Jesus or a leader in

His church and *not* stand up and take action? And with one party and candidate being the party of emancipation and the other party and candidate being the party of slavery, how could we not take political sides? In the years that followed, how could we not support Lincoln and the Republican Party and oppose Douglas and the Democratic Party? God Himself was clearly with one man, however imperfect he might be, and against the other. Who couldn't see this?

Many of us today feel the same about abortion. We look at it as a grievous evil, a monstrous transgression, a horrific crime against helpless human beings. It is the shedding of innocent blood, for profit at that. Both Hillary Clinton and Joe Biden were strong pro-abortion candidates, to the point that Hillary said in 2015 that, when it came to abortion, "deep-seated cultural codes, religious beliefs and structural biases have to be changed."[8] As for Biden, he became increasingly pro-abortion just to become the Democratic candidate. And the party platforms were as different as night and day when it came to these life-and-death issues.

As for Donald Trump, to our shock and surprise, he really became a pro-life candidate in many ways, and the three judges he appointed to the Supreme Court were instrumental in overturning the infamous *Roe v. Wade* decision of 1973, a decision that was bad law from the start. Even many liberal law scholars agreed with that assessment.[9] In stark contrast, Biden pledged to codify *Roe* as national law if the Supreme Court overturned it, and if the Democrats had sufficient control of Congress, that could well have happened. Talk about high stakes. Talk about lives being on the line. No wonder emotions ran so high.

Abortion was just one massive issue. What about the Hong

Kong protesters, risking their lives to stand up to the oppressive rule in mainland China? They looked to Trump as a hero. What about the targets of radical Islamic terror? Trump had become a shield for them. What about the teenage girl who does not want to share her locker room or bathroom with a biological male, let alone compete against him in sports? Trump had her back.[10] In contrast with all this, Biden was viewed as too friendly with China and too weak overall. He would not have moved our embassy to Jerusalem, and he sought to renew our nuclear treaty with Iran, one of the world's leading exporters of radical Islamic terror. As for the hypothetical teenage girl, Biden stood *against* her rights and sided with the trans-identified male.[11]

To repeat, no wonder emotions ran so high. No wonder so much political tension infused the air. No wonder so many Christians got caught up in a partisan political spirit.

This doesn't excuse our carnality or diminish our guilt. But it does help explain why many good people got off track. It does help explain why many fine pastors lost their perspective.

After all, isn't this exactly what happened on the other side of the political spectrum? Didn't Black Lives Matter and race issues dominate the scene? Didn't many Left-leaning Christians and many African American Christians join the gospel with politics? Wasn't Trump demonized from their pulpits and on their social media feeds because he was an alleged racist? Weren't his supporters, including his Christian supporters, branded racists too? And weren't churches judged by how they responded to the killing of George Floyd?

In some cases, believers left their churches because they were *not doing enough* politically. "You weren't vocal enough when George Floyd was killed! You failed to back the BLM movement! I thought I could depend on you, pastor, but instead you took the easy way out."

Talk about being stuck between a rock and a hard place. If you speak up, people leave. If you don't speak up, people leave. If you speak up on one side of the issue, you lose congregants. If you speak up on the other side of the issue, you lose congregants. Navigating our way through this minefield was not easy. Passions were running very high, in the name of Jesus at that. Can you better understand what happened? Can you perhaps give us another chance, recognizing that as frail human beings we failed to hit the mark?

One pastor with a multiracial church told me that the church encountered deep racial tensions for the first time ever. This occurred in the aftermath of Floyd's death. The congregation was equally divided between Black, White, and Hispanic members, and in the past, walls did not separate them. But when this pastor tried to work through the volatile issues in the news with his church, he offended people on all sides. Two White policemen, with their families, left the church, along with some Black families.

Another pastor, who is White, told me, with shock in his voice and tears, what happened in his congregation. From the start, forty years ago, it was a multiracial church and this pastor, now seventy years old, was greatly loved by his flock. But when he decided the time had come to speak openly about racial division in America, being brutally honest about the nation's past racial sins and doing his best to separate fact from fiction in the present, he suddenly lost longtime, faithful Black members.

When he went to speak with one of the men, someone he had known for decades, someone he considered a personal friend, the man was literally shaking with fear. He was genuinely afraid that this pastor was going to hurt him. To say that this White pastor, whom I know as a gentle soul, was devastated would be an understatement. At the same time, there was obviously something in this Black brother's life experience that caused these fears to surface again. To say it once more: all this has been very difficult to navigate, even for those with the best, most humble, and godly intentions. Some people, especially young people, left the church because we were too political. Others, especially young people, left because we were not political enough.

To cite one specific example of this two-sided, highly emotional controversy, after the storming of the Capitol on January 6, 2021, Evana Upshaw (herself Black/biracial), opinion editor of the student-run news site at Biola University, a strongly conservative, evangelical school in California, wrote: "Our faith, now synonymous with unwavering support for Donald Trump, is causing many to question how Christians could sell out women, immigrants, Black people, Indigenous people, people of color, the LGBTQ+ community and the poor for the sake of political power." She concluded, "Gen Z sees the hypocrisy of Christians today....It's time to pass the torch."

In response, other students referred to her comments as "propaganda," "racist and trash," "riddled with unfounded assumption and presumption." A faculty adviser then encouraged her to start publishing more conservative opinions. She, in turn, feeling exhausted and not wanting to fight, eventually transferred to a different school.[12] This is a microcosm of what we are facing in church circles and Christian schools across the nation: those in the majority not attempting to understand the lived experience of others. This has led to divisions along racial and other lines among people within the church.

Where, then, does that leave us today? How about we try for a fresh new start together? How about we agree to unite around Jesus, to major on the majors, to work on loving God, loving one another, and loving our neighbors, putting our political differences aside? Then how about we also agree to sit down and have honest discussions with each other, giving each other the right to speak freely, refusing to be easily offended, and sharing our heartfelt perspective? How about we strive for mutual understanding, self-reflection, repentance, and growth, rather than winning debates?

Millions of people in our nation really need the Lord, and we still have the answer in the gospel. Can we honor Jesus, whose last major prayer before His crucifixion was a prayer for our unity, and can we think about those who need to know Him, through us striving together for oneness? Can we demonstrate the beauty of unity through diversity rather than the ugliness of division and strife? Can we show the world what the church is really supposed to be? Now would be an ideal time.

CHAPTER 6

THE EFFECTS OF A COMPROMISED GOSPEL

PAUL PLANTED A church community in the city of Corinth, about fifty miles west of Athens, Greece. He was a spiritual father to the believers there, the one who first brought them the gospel. That's why he was so jealous for their spiritual well-being, bringing both correction and encouragement in his letters to them. In the first of those letters, he wrote, "Because of God's grace to me, I have laid the foundation like an expert builder. Now others are building on it. But whoever is building on this foundation must be very careful. For no one can lay any foundation other than the one we already have—Jesus Christ" (1 Cor. 3:10–11, NLT).

But what happens if a faulty foundation is laid? What if people build their faith on someone other than Jesus and something other than the gospel? What then? The results will be disastrous, and sooner or later a collapse will occur.

That's why Jesus was not impressed with the large crowds

that followed Him. He was looking for true, devoted, long-term disciples. That's why when He saw the throngs of people that came to hear Him, He didn't say, "I'm so glad you're here! That really blesses Me! What can I do for you?" Instead, knowing that many were following Him for the wrong reasons, He often challenged them, saying things like, "You are looking for me not because you saw the signs I performed but because you ate the loaves and had your fill." And then this radical teaching: "Very truly I tell you, unless you eat the flesh of the Son of Man and drink his blood, you have no life in you" (John 6:26, 53). Hearing these words, many of His followers walked away. This was way too much for them to absorb. Their commitment went only skin deep.

Jesus, for His part, cared for each of those people in ways beyond our understanding. He was about to give His very life for them. But He wanted to separate the true from the false, the genuine from the counterfeit. He wanted true disciples, people who understood who He was and were willing to pay the price that would be required of them in the future. He had no interest in crowds or big numbers alone. Instead, He sifted them to see what was in their hearts. (For another example, see Luke 14:25–33.)

In my book *From Holy Laughter to Holy Fire*, published in its first edition under a different title in 1995, I told the story of Scottish evangelist James Stewart, a story that seems even more relevant today than when I wrote about him almost thirty years ago.

When Stewart was just a teenager, he was offered a golden opportunity to get his message out around the world. Columbia Recording Company had already discovered a "boy gospel singer" and was beginning to widely distribute his gospel music (on vinyl records, of course). Now they wanted Stewart to record his messages and be Columbia's "boy preacher." He would preach and Columbia would get the message out to the nations. Just think of how many people could be reached! Just think of the income that could be generated! But Stewart's mother feared he wanted to accept the offer for his own glory. And then the Lord dealt with him clearly.

Stewart came to a shocking conclusion: *Satan was trying to make him into a professional evangelist.* That's right, a professional evangelist—often the contemporary American norm! How interesting it is to see that what many preachers would jump at today as a godsend, this young preacher recognized as a satanic trap. But for Stewart, God was killing ambition and the desire to be popular or make money through the Word. The Lord was preparing him for a true outpouring!

And so shortly before World War II, when Stewart was barely twenty years old, he saw revival break out in Eastern Europe. He became deeply sensitive to the difference between modern, hyped-up meetings and true visitation, really putting his finger on the problem in his little book on "Hollywood Evangelism." Speaking of our entertainment-oriented Christianity, he wrote: "The atmosphere of these meetings is so much like Hollywood that one might almost expect some comedian or film star to rush on the platform."[1] (Today, we *do* have comedians and film stars rushing to the platform; they *really* draw the masses.)

For Stewart, this was a no-compromise area. Years later he explained:

> I refuse to entertain sinners on their way to hell....I want
> to preach every time as though it were my last chance. I

do not want souls to curse my name in the lake of fire and say, "Yes, I went to such-and-such a Gospel meeting, but that preacher Stewart only entertained and joked. He made Christianity a farce!"

The old-fashioned method of evangelism was to make people weep, but the modern "Hollywood" way is to make people laugh. Everybody has to have a jolly good time....We must have plenty of jokes or it would not be a good meeting. That is why there is such a woeful lack of conviction of sin in modern evangelism. *The Holy Spirit cannot work in a frivolous atmosphere.*

And then this urgent warning:

*Here is a solemn truth that very few of God's people seem to see: Everything depends on the atmosphere of the meeting....*For example, if you were saved in a jazzy sort of atmosphere, light and frivolous, with the song leader more like a clown and the preacher merely glorifying himself and using fleshly effort, you will also turn out to be a jazzy frivolous Christian with no depth in your spiritual life.[2]

This has reached epidemic levels in our day. As expressed by Bible teacher Samuel Chadwick (1860–1932), "The Church always fails at the point of self-confidence. When the Church is run along the same lines as a circus, there may be crowds, but there is no Shekinah [meaning, manifest presence of God]."[3]

Stewart also said this: "I was once told that I would never be a very popular evangelist because I did not sufficiently 'sell my personality.' Oh, the shame! Our business is to magnify the Christ of God and not to fling about our personalities. Dr. Herbert Lockyer, in pointing out the peril of man-worship in evangelism, says, 'If a man is somewhat attractive, blessed with a fascinating personality and with power to influence multitudes, that man is often sought after rather than the Master.'"[4]

Today, with so many superstar preachers and celebrity ministers, it is all too easy for our eyes to focus on people rather than the Lord. This is a recipe for disaster, especially when the message we are hearing is not the true (or, at the least, full) gospel.

A GROWING PROBLEM IN THE CHURCH

For many years I have been deeply concerned about the type of "gospel" message people are hearing. Is it built on the Word? On truth? Does it convict people of sin (in other words, does it make them aware of their guilt before God and their need for forgiveness)? Does it offer them complete redemption through the cross? Does it tell them who Jesus really is? Does it proclaim Him as both Savior and Lord? Does it call them to repentance, telling them that following Jesus means leaving their old lives behind? Does it offer salvation as a free gift?

Throughout church history, many Christians have been hurt by a legalistic message, making their salvation a matter of works rather than of grace. This too is a fatal error. Legalism is laws without love, rules without relationship, standards without a Savior. Legalism tells people they have to work harder and become better before God will accept them, presenting a picture of the Lord as a short-tempered, petty-minded deity who is always looking to find fault and always quick to accuse. Legalism is externally imposed religion, trying to change someone from the outside in. It is extremely judgmental, normally adding other elements to the gospel and judging the salvation of others by what they do not do (as in, "Real Christians do not wear jewelry").

This gives people a false view of the Father, a false view of Jesus, a false view of the gospel, and a false view of themselves. They either think they are always unacceptable to the Lord, since they are far from perfect on their best days, or they become self-deceived, thinking they are righteous in themselves. Legalism has damaged, if not destroyed, the faith of millions of Christians over the centuries, and it remains a real danger to this day. It has driven many far away from the gospel.

But to be perfectly candid, legalism is not our biggest problem. Instead, we have gone to the opposite end of the extreme. We preach a "gospel" that calls for no repentance at all. In fact, repentance, which means turning away from sin and turning to God, all by His grace and power, is rejected as a "work." As I've heard many contemporary "believers" say when confronted with the true gospel message, "You're not going to put that bondage on me! That's religion, dude, and I don't want anything to do with that. Jesus died to set me free from your binding, dead traditions!"

This is closely related to the hyper-grace gospel,[5] one which wrongly proclaims that the moment you are born again, God pronounces your *future* sins forgiven. (Yes, Jesus died for all our sins, past, present, and future. But He does not pronounce our future sins forgiven before we commit them.) According to the hyper-grace gospel, for the rest of your life you never need to confess your sins to God since you are already forgiven in advance, and for the rest of your life the Holy Spirit will never convict you of your sins since God doesn't see your sins—ever. You can see how dangerous this doctrinal error can be, lulling Christians into a false sense of complacency, telling them that everything is fine when things are anything but fine. As for repentance, that is now reduced to "changing your mind," as in, "Listen to my teaching on this subject and change your thinking." What a serious deception.

IT GETS WORSE

Today we preach all kinds of other gospels, messages mixed with enough truth to resemble the real gospel but not enough truth to convert and transform; messages with enough Scripture to sound right but mingled with enough poison to kill. What are some of these mixed messages we hear today?

- The health and wealth gospel, promising you healing of your sicknesses and endless financial prosperity if you will only believe in Him.

- The pep-talk gospel, in which the preacher sounds more like a life coach, here to fill you with positivity, good feelings, and success.

- The celebrity gospel, which basically says, "Look, all these famous, cool people believe in Jesus. Don't you want to be cool too?"

- The progressive gospel, presenting Jesus as the enlightened teacher who is now in sync with the world.

- The social justice gospel, which reduces most topics to an issue of race and justice, with Jesus

coming to right social wrongs rather than rec-
oncile us to God.

Again, each of these messages contains a measure of truth
(you'll see that as we discuss them in greater depth), some
more and some less. But each of them falls short of proclaiming the full gospel message (some fall really short). Each
of them fails to call us to accountability for our sins, fails to
present the power of the blood of Jesus, fails to explain our
need of salvation, fails to paint a correct picture of God, and
fails to call us to holiness, by grace.

In some cases, the truth is preached first, followed by the
error, which means that a person may genuinely come to the
Lord and be born again, but because their foundation is weak
(or they built poorly on a good foundation), they never grow
strong in their relationship with God. When trials and tests
come, they are gone. They are shallow converts more than
counterfeit converts. In other cases, the error overwhelms
the truth to the point that the people think they have come
to Jesus, but in reality they are counterfeit converts. They
have never been saved at all.

On what kind of foundation is *your* faith built? What kind
of message did you hear? Who were the examples that you
followed? What does it mean to you to be born from above,
to be a follower of Jesus? And who is He to you? Your Lord
and Savior? Or simply your best buddy? Your holy enabler?
The man upstairs who gives you success? Your personalized,
supernatural concierge service? The One who makes all your
dreams come true? (Rather than a Hollywood producer, you
have a heavenly producer!) Is He the master deconstructionist,
helping you shed the myths of old-fashioned religion? Or the

angry inciter, always looking for a race-based battle to fight? Who is Jesus to you?

Without a doubt, He continues to heal the sick by His power. He has also delivered countless millions of believers from debt, bankruptcy, and poverty, providing abundantly for their needs. And many of us who follow Him are stunned to see His goodness, amazed to see what He has done with our lives, humbled to see the dreams He put in our hearts come to pass. His grace is truly amazing! And this same Jesus is also zealous to set us free from hurtful, human traditions. He too hates what many of His people have done with the Bible, turning it into a political or religious weapon, a tool to keep others under their power and influence. And He absolutely cares about justice and righteousness and stands firmly opposed to every kind of racism.

Yet none of these things, in and of themselves, come close to describing who He is and why we need Him. None of these emphases brings us to a place of conviction, repentance, and surrender. Consequently, to the extent we have imbibed any of these "gospel" messages, especially in our initial, formative stages, is the extent to which we need to rebuild our spiritual foundations.

In 2013 I wrote an article titled "A Compromised Gospel Produces Compromised Fruit,"[6] saying:

This is where we find ourselves today:

- A senior editor of one of the nation's leading Christian publications speaks with regret of "the long-standing evangelical myth that there should be something different about the Christian."[7]

- A glamorous spokeswoman for conservative Christian values explains that, "I am a Christian, and I am a model. Models pose for pictures, including lingerie and swimwear photos."[8]

- A well-known rapper claims a conversion to Christianity and states, "I love God, Jesus Christ is my savior and I'm still out here thuggin'." He has been baptized, attends church regularly and says, "I still love the strip club and I still smoke and drink. I'm faithful to my family, so I wanted to make an album where you could love God and be of God, but still get it poppin' in your life."[9]

Things have gone downhill since then.

THE HEALTH AND WEALTH GOSPEL

When I came to faith in 1971, I was taught that God still healed today and that it was right to pray for the sick. Along the way I saw some amazing answers to prayer. Yes, God still heals! And the Bible seemed pretty clear to me on the subject too. But as the years passed and I did not see the miracles I was expecting to see—such as lame people walking or blind people seeing—I began to question what I believed, eventually joining another church.

There, I became completely skeptical about divine healing to the point of reading books that taught *against* healing and miracles for today. I even wrote a paper for the pastor stating that in the Bible God did a lot more smiting than healing. And when my sister-in-law was miraculously healed at a gospel rally in New York, a sign to her that God wanted to heal everyone, I flatly rejected her testimony, saying, "Well, Joni Eareckson prayed for God to work in her life and she ended up with a broken neck, wheelchair-bound for life." That's how hardened I had become.

Then, as the Holy Spirit got hold of me in 1982, bringing me to repentance for my pride, I began to hear testimonies of people being healed. But their theology was all wrong! At least, that's what I thought. So I said to myself, "I have the right theology, but I'm not seeing anyone healed. They have the wrong theology, and they are getting healed. Something is not lining up."

That's part of what prompted me to change the subject of my doctoral thesis for my PhD in Near Eastern Languages and Literatures from New York University, writing on the subject "I Am the LORD Your Healer: A Philological Study of the Root *RAPA'* in the Hebrew Bible and the Ancient Near East."[10] I completed this in 1985, and in 1995 Zondervan published my book *Israel's Divine Healer* (it contains 165,000 words, 80,000 words of text and 85,000 words of endnotes, so it is anything but a light read). I also wrote lengthy articles on the root *RAPA'* for the leading theological dictionaries of Old Testament words. To put it simply, I have really studied this subject closely!

Based on the Bible, not experience, I concluded that healing and health were God's ideal will for His obedient children, that it is right to pray for healing and to expect healing, that the gifts of healing are still for today, and that our healing was paid for on the cross. As for the subject of "wealth," I also believe that there are many promises in the Bible that God rewards generosity with generosity and that He honors us financially as we honor Him financially. At the same time, *I categorically reject the carnal prosperity message, and I believe there is great error in the contemporary "health and wealth, name it and claim it" gospel.*

I categorically reject the message "Jesus died to make you financially rich!" I reject the notion that wealth is proof of divine blessing while poverty is proof of divine disfavor. To the contrary, some of the wickedest people on earth are wealthy and some of the godliest are poor. And I categorically reject the idea that health is proof of divine blessing and sickness is proof of divine disfavor. To the contrary, some of the wickedest people on earth are healthy and some of the godliest are sick.

To be clear, I do not believe that God *blesses* someone with sickness, and I do believe that health is often a blessing from above. Nor is poverty, in and of itself, a good thing. Certainly, being poor is not proof that you are close to God!

But the health and wealth gospel is a massive distortion of biblical truth, setting people up for false expectations and deep disappointment the moment their bubble is burst. "I thought everything was supposed to go well for me as a believer!" Not only so, but it does not confront sinners with their sin, nor does it call them to repentance, nor does it explain the meaning of the cross. Instead, believing in Jesus is the guaranteed method to make all your troubles disappear. Ask Him in, and you will be healthy and wealthy for life! What a ridiculous, unbiblical message.

That's why I devoted one chapter in *Has God Failed You?* to the subject "Perhaps It Was Wrong Theology That Failed You?" Tragically, because many people think that the health and wealth gospel *is* the gospel—in other words, it's the only message they heard, and it's the way they have understood the Bible and the way they relate to God—when the fairy tale story is disrupted by serious illness or financial challenge, they reject God entirely. Perhaps this is what happened to you or someone close to you?

The solution? Go back to the Bible and rediscover who God is and what the gospel is. Then, on that solid foundation and with right expectations, you can build a solid spiritual life.

THE PEP-TALK GOSPEL

Some years ago, while flipping through channels on TV, I heard a very persuasive, very likeable, even inspirational speaker. But as I listened, I couldn't tell if it was a real estate investor telling you how you could become rich with his techniques, a motivational speaker giving you his keys to success in life, or a contemporary preacher. I kid you not. That's how much "the gospel" has been watered down in some circles. "Are you feeling down and discouraged? God wants to put a smile on your face and a little pep in your step!"

Of course, in the midst of our teaching and preaching, we bring words of encouragement and hope. We talk about a God who brings joy and peace. We share testimonies of people who have been delivered from depression and fear. And we proclaim loudly and clearly, "God is good all the time! All the time, God is good!" And it is true. Every single word of it.

But once again, this is not the heart and soul of the gospel. This is not the message of salvation and transformation. Instead, it is part of the fruit of walking with God, part of the encouragement we received from fellowship with Him. But there is nothing salvific—meaning, "saving"—in the pep-talk gospel, nothing that exposes the sinner's guilt, nothing that would cause them to run to the cross for mercy, nothing that would lead them to repentance, and nothing that would transform their innermost being.

Instead, it is like putting a colorful bandage on a cancer patient or giving a candy-coated aspirin to someone with gangrene. The bandage might look pretty and the aspirin might taste good, but neither will heal the cancer or get rid of the gangrene. They will only distract from the real, deadly issues at hand.

As I wrote in my 2018 book *Playing With Holy Fire*:

> What exactly is the pep-talk gospel? It is a feel-good, motivational message, and nothing more. It lifts you up and cheers you up and puts a smile on your face without ever calling you to turn from sin, without ever confronting you with the consequences of disobedience, without ever talking about judgment or God's wrath. That is not the gospel.
>
> According to this gospel, sadness is your adversary, not sin. Depression is your enemy, not depravity. Jesus doesn't want you to feel bad, but He's not calling you to turn from sin. That is the pep-talk gospel. Happiness, not holiness, is the goal.[11]

I added, "Like many of you, I've been a student of the Word for decades, and I've gone through the New Testament over and over again. So here's a simple challenge to my fellow lovers of the Word: Please show me this pep-talk message anywhere in the Scriptures. Please show it to me in the words of Jesus or Paul or John or Peter or Jacob (James) or Judah (Jude). Please show it to me in the words of Moses or the prophets or the Psalms or Proverbs. Please show it to me in the Word of God."[12] It simply is not there.

By all means, be encouraged in the Lord. By all means, walk in His joy and peace. By all means, proclaim His goodness, believe in His goodness, and revel in His goodness. But preach the rest of the message first and foremost. Then add these wonderful truths to the solid foundation of your faith. Putting a smile on your face and being positive is not the same as being forgiven, cleansed, born again, and transformed.

THE CELEBRITY GOSPEL

Long ago, it was anything but cool to be a follower of Jesus. Instead, following the Master meant rejection, hardship, persecution, and opposition—and in some cases, even death. This was especially true if you were a leader in the movement. You were often singled out for attack. As Paul wrote about the suffering of the apostles, "To this very hour we go hungry and thirsty, we are in rags, we are brutally treated, we are homeless. We work hard with our own hands. When we are cursed, we bless; when we are persecuted, we endure it; when we are slandered, we answer kindly. We have become the scum of the earth, the garbage of the world—right up to this moment" (1 Cor. 4:11–13).

Because of this, no one had to explain to you what Jesus meant when said to His would-be followers, "If anyone would come after me, let him deny himself and take up his cross and follow me. For whoever would save his life will lose it, but whoever loses his life for my sake and the gospel's will save it" (Mark 8:34–35, ESV). And this: "The student is not above the teacher, nor a servant above his master. It is enough for students to be like their teachers, and servants like their masters.

If the head of the house has been called Beelzebul, how much more the members of his household" (Matt. 10:24–25)! And this: "If the world hates you, keep in mind that it hated me first. If you belonged to the world, it would love you as its own. As it is, you do not belong to the world, but I have chosen you out of the world. That is why the world hates you. Remember what I told you: 'A servant is not greater than his master.' If they persecuted me, they will persecute you also. If they obeyed my teaching, they will obey yours also" (John 15:18–20).

Today things have shifted dramatically. The pastor must look cool. The worship team must look cool. And, of course, Jesus must be the epitome of cool. "You can be cool too! Just ask Jesus in! He would be honored to accept your invitation."

Better still, "So-and-so, a famous celebrity, is following Jesus these days as well. You can be in the same spiritual club as them!"

Of course, we don't say it quite like that. But you can be sure that Jesus has become part of a slickly marketed package, one designed to produce consumers rather than disciples. This too is destined to fall.

To be clear, I don't believe that we're supposed to be *uncool*. Or that it's wrong for a worship team to coordinate their colors. Or that the pastor needs to be eighty years old, bald, portly, and reading from the King James Bible (with the help of some massive reading glasses). Not at all.

It is the appeal to cool that is the problem. It is the fact that the "gospel" cannot be presented without all these other trappings. It is putting forth an image that appeals to pride and worldliness. That is where the problem lies.

Digging deeper, there is something wrong in the whole mindset behind this "celebrity Christianity." As I wrote in

How Saved Are We? in 1990, beginning with this quote from A. W. Tozer:

> "The trouble is the whole 'Accept Christ' attitude is likely to be wrong. It shows Christ applying to us rather than us to Him. It makes Him stand hat-in-hand awaiting our verdict on Him, instead of our kneeling with troubled hearts awaiting His verdict on us. It may even permit us to accept Christ by an impulse of mind or emotions, painlessly, at no loss to our ego and no inconvenience to our usual way of life." But Jesus and the old life don't mix. We are called to press upward to Him.
>
> How would a young man feel after he proposed to the woman he loved if she looked at him and said: "Yes, I'll marry you. But do I have to give up my other boyfriends? Will you want me back home every night? Can I still sleep around and have fun?" What would his reaction be? He would be hurt and disappointed. He would be deeply shattered and shocked. He expected her unswerving loyalty. He wanted a true mate for life.
>
> What about Jesus our heavenly Bridegroom? Does He deserve less than that? Will He accept sinners if they do not pledge Him their loyalty? Yet we are afraid to tell the unregenerate that they must give up their "other lovers" if they want to be joined to Him. We don't want to turn them off! What a pitiful mentality.

And then this striking story:

> In the late 1950s Mickey Cohen, a notorious gangster, attended a Billy Graham meeting in Beverly Hills. Although he expressed some interest in the message, he "made no commitment until some time later when

another friend urged him, using Revelation 3:20 as a warrant, to invite Jesus Christ into his life. This he professed to do, but his life subsequently gave no evidence of repentance, 'that mighty change of mind, heart and life' [Trench]. He rebuked [his] friend, telling him: 'You did not tell me that I would have to give up my work,' meaning his rackets; 'You did not tell me that I would have to give up my friends,' meaning his gangster associates. He had heard that so-and-so was a Christian football player, so-and-so a Christian cowboy, so-and-so a Christian actress, so-and-so a Christian senator, and he really thought that he could be a Christian gangster. Alas, there was not evidence of repentance. Many have sadly forgotten that the only evidence of the new birth is the new life. The real problem is that some evangelists, like some converts, have failed to realize that the fault lies in the defective message" (J. Edwin Orr).[13]

Today, the number of defective messages preached in our churches in America has reached epidemic levels, especially with so much unfiltered material coming our way through social media. Anyone can get a message out, virtually without scrutiny and without accountability, and once that message goes viral, it's almost impossible to control the damage.

That's why in my 2021 book *Revival or We Die: A Great Awakening Is Our Only Hope*, I devoted a chapter to the subject "From Amazing Grace to Amazing Sinners." There I noted that:

The more clearly we see the depth of our sin, the more clearly we see the breadth of God's mercy. The more we realize the wretched nature of our rebellion, the more we understand the amazing nature of God's grace.

Yet today, we don't like to talk about coming to God

as "wretches." That hurts our self-esteem! And rather than telling sinners how amazing the Lord's grace is, we tell them how amazing *they are.* No wonder there is so little conviction of sin today. No wonder there are so many shallow conversions—if they be conversions at all. No wonder there is so little depth in so much of the contemporary American church....

The biblical gospel proclaims that human beings are terribly sinful and that God's grace is truly amazing. The American gospel proclaims that lost sinners are truly amazing and that any talk of God's judgment is really terrible. As for God's grace, it's like icing on the cake for the sinner—and be assured that the sinner's cake is already quite beautiful and wonderful. God just wants to add some special ingredients to make it taste even better.[14]

This is not the gospel. It will not save, and it will not transform.

It is true that the Lord loves us with an intensity we cannot imagine. It is true that He offers us a close, wonderful, and intimate relationship with Him and that, as His children, He really enjoys spending time with us. That is totally mind-boggling! But the way of the cross is not the way of worldly fame and success, nor is following Jesus cool or hip, nor is God honored to have us in His family. We've got the whole thing turned upside down.

THE PROGRESSIVE GOSPEL

The next version of the "gospel" is the progressive "woke" gospel, one that seeks to win the world by becoming like the world (or one that sincerely believes that leftist social values are in harmony with the Bible). When it comes to abortion, this "gospel" agrees with the world: "This is all about women's rights! This is about reproductive care. This is about body autonomy. Jesus stands with these women and against those fundamentalist fanatics."

When it comes to same-sex "marriage" and LGBTQ+ talking points, this "gospel" leads the way, saying that Jesus came for the outcast and the marginalized, that God is love and love is love, and that the Lord would never judge us because of who we love, that there is neither male nor female in Christ, and therefore it is fine to be transgender or queer or nonbinary, that the church has misused the Bible to prohibit same-sex relationships, just as the church previously misused the Bible to sanction slavery, segregation, and the oppression of women. It's time to get liberated from right-wing, mean-spirited, judgmental religion and discover the real Jesus!

As for this Jesus, He didn't die for our sins as much as die to set an example of selfless love. Let us follow in His footsteps and do the same.

Again, there are some truths in this so-called gospel. We *are* called to reach out to the marginalized. We *are* called to demonstrate sacrificial love. We *are* called to love our neighbor as ourselves, whomever that neighbor may be. And it is true that every human being, regardless of how they live or identify, is created in the image of God. It is true that Jesus died for every single person on the planet, whether they identify as trans, bi, queer, gay, or straight. It's also true that, all too often, the world hears a message of condemnation and exclusion from the church, a self-righteous message that is selective in what sins it confronts and what sins it overlooks. Guilty here, as charged.

But the biblical gospel also goes against the grain of the world and will always be rejected as antiquated and out-moded—as anything but progressive. Let's not fool ourselves.

THE SOCIAL JUSTICE GOSPEL

Closely related to the progressive gospel is the social justice gospel. In this version of the "gospel" Jesus is an angry prophet who is focused on the issues of racial equality and social justice, overturning the tables of America's White status quo. He preaches against systemic racism, White privilege, and police brutality and is committed to seeing equal outcomes as well as equal opportunities. Anything less than this is unacceptable.

He is the Black Lives Matter movement quoting Scripture, the liberator of all oppressed classes (including all people of color and all sexual minorities). And He is calling the White church to account for its past and present religious hypocrisy, holding all White Christians responsible for the nation's past and present sins against African Americans.

Following Him does not simply mean not being racist. It means being "antiracist." It means teaching your children that White Christians are part of the historic oppressor class. It means taking on guilt because of your privileged status. It even means feeling shame if you are a White American Christian. That is now the heart and soul of the gospel. As for the cross, it is presented as a symbol of what the oppressor class does to God's people. Or is it Jesus nailing White supremacy to the tree?

This "gospel" is almost the polar opposite of the "gospel" of Christian nationalism, which we addressed in chapter 5, the mixed gospel message that wraps the cross in the flag.[15] Jesus, above all, is a patriot! So yes, there are dangerous extremes

119

on every side. But what they all have in common is that they fundamentally distort the gospel, thereby robbing the cross of its power.

In this case, the social justice gospel rightly affirms God's abhorrence of slavery and segregation, and it recognizes that doing justice and caring for the poor are major themes throughout the Bible. But it makes a secondary issue the main issue, it fails to preach redemption and reconciliation and forgiveness and transformation, and it stirs up hatred and strife rather than helping us find true unity in Jesus.

What happens to those who embrace messages like these we have discussed in this chapter? If one of these messages is the foundation on which they (or you) have built their spiritual lives, then they most likely have never been born from above. If they (or you) embraced one of these messages after coming to faith, then they are either out of balance, very superficial, or drifting further away from the Lord. Either way, the solution is simple: back to the biblical gospel! We have all sinned and are guilty before God, deserving of condemnation. But rather than condemn us, God sent His Son Jesus to take our place on the cross, dying for our sins and then rising from the dead on the third day. If we acknowledge our guilt, cry out to God for mercy, believe that Jesus died for us and rose again, asking the Lord to save us from our sins and give us a new heart, He will do it. As surely as He is God, He will meet you, forgive you, and change you. Count on it.

CHAPTER 7

"BECAUSE INIQUITY
WILL ABOUND"

Speaking about a time of extreme apostasy, Jesus said, "Because lawlessness will abound, the love of many will grow cold" (Matt. 24:12, NKJV; the KJV used the word "iniquity" instead of "lawlessness"; it is *anomia* in Greek). In other words, because sin and lawlessness will be so ubiquitous, many believers will turn away from the Lord. It will be much harder to do what is right and much easier to do what is wrong. As a result, large numbers of believers will renounce or lose their faith. It's like saying, "Because the thunderstorms will be so heavy, lots of people will get wet."

Now, you may recall that earlier in the book I said that although I don't believe we are in *the specific time of falling away* that Jesus spoke of—meaning, the time of the final apostasy and rebellion—we are in *a similar time*, a time of great temptation, a time of increasing challenges to our faith. At times like this, it makes perfect spiritual sense that more and more people will be turning away from the Lord. The greater the battle, the greater the casualties, and the greater the temptations, the greater the moral failures.

Let's think of this in practical, everyday terms. You want to spend a week in fasting, Bible study, and prayer, so you rent an isolated cabin in the woods with no Wi-Fi, cell phone signal, or TV and with only bottles of water in the fridge. And the cabin is several hours from the nearest town. In that setting there's a good chance you will achieve your goals. What else do you have to do?

Now let's change the picture. The cabin is stocked with all your favorite meals and snacks, it has high-speed Wi-Fi and a great cell signal, not to mention a seventy-two-inch TV with every imaginable cable channel, including porn channels and pay-per-view sports. And some of the best restaurants in the city are just five minutes away, plus there are $100 gift cards for each restaurant waiting for you in the cabin. It would be much harder to spend that week in prayer, Bible study, and fasting. Wouldn't you agree?

It's the same with our world today. No generation in history has had so many distractions to deal with. No generation in history has had so many temptations. No generation in history has had so much entertainment and defilement available right at their fingertips (quite literally). That means it is much harder to live consecrated, undistracted lives for the Lord, lives that are free from the contamination of sin and the saturation of the world. Yet the Word of God calls us to keep ourselves from being polluted by the world.[1]

To say it bluntly, we are in the midst of a fierce war for our souls, yet many of us are living as if we were on vacation. We must wake up! The enemy of our souls is out for our souls. Make no mistake about it. Sadly, as A. W. Tozer wrote more than sixty years ago, "The idea that this world is a playground instead of a battleground has now been accepted in practice by the vast majority of fundamentalist [evangelical] Christians."[2]

This is not to minimize the terrible suffering endured for the faith by our brothers and sisters in heavily persecuted countries. They are paying the ultimate price for their convictions, right until this day. But in this context, I'm simply speaking of the temptations of sin and the distractions of the world. We are facing these in unique and unprecedented ways, because of which many more are falling away from the Lord. This is a simple observation rather than rocket science.

So in addition to the objections of the new atheists and the agnostic professors, in addition to the impact of LGBTQ+ activism, in addition to the problem of suffering, in addition to the many church scandals, in addition to the challenge of religious exclusivism, there is now one more great obstacle to our relationship with the Lord: lots and lots of opportunities to sin. Some things just never change.

THE AGE-OLD PROBLEM OF SIN

There's an old saying that either sin will keep you from the Bible, or the Bible will keep you from sin. The same can be said about prayer. Either sin will keep you from prayer, or prayer will keep you from sin. In both cases, the more that sin is present, the more that devotion to God will be absent. It's a simple spiritual principle.

It's also true that distractions will keep us from maturing in the Lord. Jesus addressed this in the parable of the sower, which speaks about a man sowing seed on different types of ground. (The man in the parable represents Jesus, and the seed represents God's Word.) The seed that falls on thorny soil grows into a plant, but the thorns choke it, and so it cannot come to maturity and bear fruit.

What do these thorns represent? As Jesus explained, they represent the cares of the world, the deceitfulness of riches, the pleasures of life, and the desires for other things that enter in and choke the Word, and it proves unfruitful. (See Matthew 13:22; Mark 4:19; Luke 8:14). We live in a very thorny world!

That's why John wrote 1 John 2:15–17: "Do not love the world or the things in the world. If anyone loves the world, the love of the Father is not in him. For all that is in the world—the desires of the flesh and the desires of the eyes and pride of life—is not from the Father but is from the world. And the world is passing away along with its desires, but whoever does the will of God abides forever" (ESV). In our day, it has become increasingly difficult to keep our hearts free from the love of the world.

Think back to the days before we had cable TV, let alone streaming services online. We had four or five channels to choose from, and some of them stopped broadcasting at midnight. And for many years, our home TVs were black and white, often with poor reception. Before that, there was radio only, and before that, only books and table games and the like.

Contrast that way of life with today's way of life, when you can watch breaking news on your cell phone or view an endless number of movies or a multitude of live sporting events—almost wherever you are in the world and right in the palm of your hand. And let's not forget the constant distraction of endless texts, messages, emails, and social media posts. Our brains are becoming rewired for constant digital stimulation, to the point that it's becoming increasingly difficult to focus for long. This too is destructive to our spiritual life. It is so much easier to be shallow and scattered than to be deep and focused.

Then there are the overt seductions of sin, none more pervasive than that of pornography. This is an especially acute problem in light of the frequent warnings in Scripture about the destructive power of sexual sin. This is a problem that has been here throughout human history, and no one warned about it more extensively and vividly than King Solomon in the Book of Proverbs. Yet, as Nehemiah stated, "Among the many nations there was no king like him, and he was beloved by his God, and God made him king over all Israel. Nevertheless, foreign women made even him to sin" (Neh. 13:26, ESV). Of course, the temptations not only go both ways, meaning, male to female and female to male, but these days they go in every conceivable direction.

Let's say, then, that pornography was a real temptation in your life, but you were born in 1955, as I was. If you were sixteen years old and wanted to look at porn, you would have to know someone who could buy a porn magazine. Perhaps the father of one of your friends subscribed to *Playboy*. You were too young to go into a porn theater, if one was even in your town, and in all likelihood you certainly could not walk into some burlesque theater to watch live porn (unless you lived in a big city, for instance). And even if you got hold of a copy of *Playboy*, it would have been limited to some nude pictures.

Compare that scenario with life today, when kids are getting exposed to porn as young as eight years old and when virtually any type of pornographic image or scene can be accessed by anyone on a cell phone, tablet, or PC.[3] You can even go online and chat directly with another person who will strip and perform for you. Talk about a much more dangerous and difficult situation. Talk about an exponential increase in temptation. Talk about a massive, demonically designed trap.

Now think back to those lines about sin keeping you from the Bible and prayer, or the Bible and prayer keeping you from sin. Porn has severed many a man (and woman) from fellowship with God. Porn has consumed many an hour that was meant for prayer, family time, or constructive activities. Porn has contributed to many a divorce. Porn has destroyed many a ministry. Porn has polluted and defiled many a life and condemned many a conscience.

This is another reason why many have fallen away from the faith: the pull of sin was too strong, the discouragement too deep, the degeneration too dark. Yet this is just one example of what can happen when "lawlessness abounds." And note carefully what Jesus said would follow: "The love of many will grow cold" (Matt. 24:12, NLT).

How could it not grow cold when that fiery love was doused with sexual pollution, when countless hours were spent surfing the web for more, when unclean thoughts filled the mind and guilt flooded the heart? Of course there will be backsliding, sometimes to the point of complete apostasy. At best, there will be divided hearts, undisciplined lives, lukewarmness, and lack of effectiveness—and that is at best.

TOO FAT TO FLY

I related this story in the book *Breaking the Stronghold of Food*. It may sound out of place here in this book, but I'll explain in a moment:

The words were spoken clearly, carefully, and with great conviction: "Brethren, we are too fat to fly."

It was a Sunday night late in 1982 and we had gathered to pray together for a few hours in the midst of a wonderful spiritual visitation that our congregation was experiencing. These Sunday night prayer meetings had become the highlight of the week as we would come together in great anticipation, not knowing what would happen as we prayed.

Lost sinners came to faith during the prayer meeting. Sick bodies were healed. Believers came to deep repentance and were mightily filled with the Spirit.

But this particular night, something was missing. The meeting was flat, lacking vitality, and there was a heaviness in the air. That's when one of the men there spoke those words: "Brethren, we are too fat to fly. We've had our nice, big meals today before coming here, and now we're so full of food that we're tired and lethargic."

Put another way, you can't walk in the Spirit if you indulge the flesh, and that's exactly what we had done that night. Like an overgorged bird, we were too fat to fly.[4]

Today, as America becomes more and more decadent morally and spiritually, our nation also becomes more and more decadent in terms of diet. But poor eating habits also contribute to our spiritual lethargy, dulling our senses, increasing our addictions, and making us slaves of the flesh in the most fundamental way, namely slaves to our bellies. This is another aspect to the challenge of this age.

Of course, we recognize that gluttony and obesity hinder us physically. Or does anyone really think that a 400-pound man could be a top pole vaulter, or a 300-pound woman could be a top sprinter or long-distance runner? In the same way, if we overindulge our flesh, we will starve (or, at the least, diminish) the spiritual side of our beings.

Today, as we have become more sedentary as a society and more given to junk food diets, we have become less disciplined. This affects our spiritual lives too and is directly related to our larger cultural decadence, which is reflected in our restaurant menus (featuring desserts such as "Death by Chocolate") and with portions that dwarf those in other countries. We are virtually drugging ourselves with unhealthy food, making us lethargic and subjecting us to a wide range of debilitating illnesses.

This aspect of our spiritual warfare is certainly much less overt than, say, the attack of pornography or illicit drugs, since we need to eat in order to live. Yet it is another obstacle we must overcome in this decadent age. Devotion to the Lord requires discipline, and if we can't control our physical appetites, it's unlikely that we will master the other areas of our lives.

THE ADDICTIONS NEVER END

Another area of concern is the rise of gambling addictions in America, something that came to my attention while casually watching some sports. Betting odds were being announced and updated through the sporting event, and gambling apps and websites were being advertised throughout the show. "Surely," I thought, "this cannot be good."

When I decided to research things in more depth, I came across article after article talking about the dangerous rise of gambling in America. One article in particular got my attention, published on July 11, 2022 (the very day I was writing my own article on gambling addiction). It started with this jarring headline: "'We've seen people go from six-figure incomes...to living on the streets': Why it's easier than ever to get addicted to gambling. Experts say there needs to be more education and awareness around this 'invisible addiction.'"[5]

Chew on that for a moment: going "from six-figure incomes... to living on the streets," all because of gambling. Isn't this cause for concern?

The article's author, Serah Lewis, explained that gambling access has increased since 2018 "when the Supreme Court overturned a decision that limited sports betting to Nevada," creating an environment for gambling ads and apps to pop "up everywhere since."

Lewis went on to report, "More than two dozen states have legalized sports betting in the past few years. And according to a report by the American Gaming Association, sports betting and iGaming revenue grew by double digit percentages in April from the previous year."

The article went on to state that Kevin Whyte, the executive director of the National Council on Problem Gambling, told *Newsweek* in a 2022 interview that "his organization saw a 45% increase in gambling hotline calls and a 100% increase in text and chat communications in the first year after the Supreme Court decision.

"'We believe that the expansion of online gambling, including sports betting, has increased the severity and rate of gambling problems,' Whyte said."[6] And that expansion amounted to more than fifty billion dollars in 2021.[7]

This too is yet one more obstacle to overcome and one more temptation to avoid. Iniquity and lawlessness really are abounding.

ANOTHER EFFECT OF "LAWLESSNESS"

As explained at the beginning of this chapter, the Greek word *anomia* (found in Matthew 24:12) refers to "wickedness" as well as lawlessness.[8] This concept suggests that the sinful attitudes of the culture challenge our walks with the Lord as well. That's because it is so much easier to swim with the tide, to embrace the prevailing culture, to go with the flow, rather than to push back and resist.

If you decide not to acquiesce to the latest LGBTQ+ talking points on the job or in school, you will be vilified, marginalized, and demonized. You will be excluded, marked, mocked, and even canceled. You will be branded a bigot, a hater, a Nazi, to the point of losing promotions, jobs, scholarships, and your reputation. Who wants any of this? Better to conform than to resist. At the least, better to be silent. That's certainly what the flesh wants to do.

Yet when we do this, compromising our convictions for the sake of our comfort, we compromise our very souls. This too is part of the Lord's warning, and it accurately describes the culture of the day. Lawlessness abounds. Wickedness has increased. The opposition to holiness is mounting. The resistance to the gospel is growing.

Will we stand tall for the world to see, or will we cower? Will we hold to God's truth regardless of cost or consequence, or will we rationalize our spineless choices? Will we have the courage to do what is right even when it makes us unpopular, or will we succumb to the pressure to conform? Put another way, which is more important to us, being accepted by God or being accepted by people? Whose favor do we value more? Whose praise do we live for?

In the words of Paul, "Am I now trying to win the approval of human beings, or of God? Or am I trying to please people? If I were still trying to please people, I would not be a servant of Christ" (Gal. 1:10). That is some straightforward language. In that same spirit, Jesus said to religious leaders in His day, "How can you believe since you accept glory from one another but do not seek the glory that comes from the only God" (John 5:44)? As John recorded later in this same book, "Yet at the same time many even among the leaders believed in him [referring to Jesus]. But because of the Pharisees they would not openly acknowledge their faith for fear they would be put out of the synagogue; for they loved human praise more than praise from God" (John 12:42–43).

Some of you reading these words just felt an arrow pierce your heart. I have felt that same arrow too! May the Lord open our eyes to eternal realities and deliver us from the fear of man and the desire to be praised by man. As a colleague of mine once said, "When you are on your knees, the praise and the criticism go right over your head."

Or perhaps this question will help us get the right perspective: Would you rather be rejected by God or by people? Chew on that for a moment. How you answer that question will have eternal repercussions.

PUSHING AGAINST THE TIDAL WAVE OF SIN AND TEMPTATION

Have you ever heard the saying "being forewarned is being forearmed"? When you know the hurricane is coming, you board up your house and go to safer territory. When you know a severe cold spell is on the way, you make sure that you have proper winter clothing. In the same way, the Bible not only predicts seasons of great temptation and lawlessness, it also tells us how to survive such times. We can even *thrive* during such difficult seasons, with the grace and help of God. In fact, the same proven methods for overcoming sin and resisting temptation that apply to everyday life also apply in times of severe pressure and stress. We just need to be more vigilant in putting these methods into practice during times like this.

Consider this important biblical principle: when you are struggling with an area of sin and disobedience, don't cut things back, cut them off. For example, if you're a married person who is getting pulled into an adulterous relationship, trying to resist and yet seeing your resolve lessen by the day, you have only one solution: cut it off! Don't trick yourself into thinking, "We'll just cut back on some of our contact. We won't text each other so much or talk so much on the phone. And we won't see each other face to face as much." That will never work. Never.

Instead, as long as you leave that door open, the temptation will grow in intensity until you end up crossing a very dangerous, forbidden line. Your only choice is to cut the relationship off, even if it means finding a different job (if you're coworkers) or making clear to the other person that you can never text, call, email, or see each other alone again.

For this reason, Jesus used such strong language when warning us about the power of sinful strongholds, telling us to gouge out the eye that caused us to sin or cut off the hand or foot that led us to sin.[9] Of course, as His hearers understood (and understand to this day), He was not talking about mutilating our bodies, since, in fact, our eyes, hands, or feet are not the problem. It's our hearts and minds that are the problem. It's the choices we make that get us into trouble. Our eyes or limbs only follow those choices.

Still, the message is clear: we must deal ruthlessly and radically with sin. Otherwise, it will deal ruthlessly and radically with us.

In the same way, parents need to be especially vigilant in raising children in this environment. One mother poured out her heart to me, telling me the path her eighteen-year-old daughter was on, now identifying as a boy, getting testosterone shots, and breaking off all contact with her parents. This mother, a longtime friend of our family, wrote:

> I think so much of our problem today is media in general. It opens children's eyes to things they have no idea how to handle. I remember my daughter as a tween and young teen very into cosplay, dressing up as different characters and getting photos. I thought nothing of it, only that she was artistic and creative.
>
> When I see some people's stories, the story was exact to mine. There were things I didn't know led to other things, but looking back and now knowing this trend, it all came from somewhere. Someone is pushing this. And it literally made me feel sick yesterday when I watched Matt Walsh's video [about young people self-diagnosing themselves as having psychological conditions such as multiple personality disorder] and thought "Who on earth is making this content?!? And making it so appealing to kids?!!!!"
>
> I'm older and wiser and these kids have no internet, no smartphone, nothing. Yes, they are the oddball. But I was too naive and didn't know what was out there. I don't believe that many believers do, since we didn't grow up in the digital age. I feel like I'm always one step behind. I am much more informed now and realize

what can lead where. I just hope it isn't too late for many parents out there dealing with these issues.[10]

We must be much more vigilant today, much more on the alert, much more focused on what our kids are learning and taking in, on what kinds of influences are affecting their thinking. Today is not like yesterday.

Another biblical principle of great importance in times like this is *always remembering the final end, the final consequences*. It is derived from the Hebrew word *acharit* (pronounced *ah-kha-reet*), which means that which comes after; after-effects; final consequences; end. It is a theme I have preached on for decades, and it is a theme that has literally saved my life.

The principle is simple: from our normal vantage point, we cannot see someone's back. We don't see what comes after. And so if I tore the back of my expensive suit jacket, leaving a gaping hole, you would never know it if you only saw me from the front. From that angle, I would look fine. But as soon as I walked past you, you would gasp. Moments ago, everything seemed great. But when you saw my back, the whole picture changed. Instead of looking sharp, I looked sloppy. And that's the biblical principle: from our ordinary human vantage point, we cannot see that which comes after, the final consequences of a matter, the *acharit*.

But God always sees the whole picture. In His eyes, the *acharit* is always in full view. And if we are to live holy lives, we must gain His perspective. In a moment, this will all become clear.

This word *acharit* occurs sixty-one times in the Old Testament, but thirteen of those times—20 percent of the total—it is found in the Book of Proverbs. There is a lesson here! In fact, the whole purpose of Proverbs can be summed up in one verse, Proverbs 19:20, which I translate as: "Listen to counsel and receive discipline/instruction so that you will be wise in your final end" (literally, "in your *acharit*"). That's what really counts. When all is said and done, you will have acted and lived wisely. Your *acharit* will be blessed.

The problem is that Satan never shows us the *acharit*. Instead, he is completely focused on the here and now, on the pleasure of the moment, on the need of the hour. So he does his best to get our eyes off the *acharit*, the "end" of the story. Just think of Esau, who sold his lifelong birthright for one meal just because he was hungry at that moment.

> Once when Jacob was cooking a stew, Esau came in from the open, famished. And Esau said to Jacob, "Give me some of that red stuff to gulp down, for I am famished"—which is why he was named Edom. Jacob said, "First sell me your birthright." And Esau said, "I am at the point of death, so of what use is my birthright to me?" But Jacob said, "Swear to me first." So he swore to him, and sold his birthright to Jacob. Jacob then gave Esau bread and lentil stew; he ate and drank, and he rose and went away. Thus did Esau spurn the birthright.
> —Genesis 25:29–34, JPS TANAKH

Hebrews exhorts us *not* to be like this "godless" man, "who for a single meal sold his inheritance rights as the oldest son. Afterward, as you know, when he wanted to inherit this blessing, he was rejected. Even though he sought the blessing with tears, he could not change what he had done" (Heb. 12:16–17). His *acharit* was miserable.

One time, after disobeying the Lord in a relatively minor way, I felt grieved and said to myself, *"Before* I yield to sin next time, I need to remember how I felt *after* I sinned this time." That would be the antidote. But everything in our fallen nature works against that *acharit* vision. It says, "Forget about the consequences. Just think about *now*." God says, "Focus on the *acharit!*" Take practical steps. Extreme temptation requires extreme resistance.[11]

One key way we can resist is by fleeing from the bad stuff and pursuing the good stuff. As Paul wrote to Timothy, "Flee the evil desires of youth and pursue righteousness, faith, love and peace, along with those who call on the Lord out of a pure heart" (2 Tim. 2:22). If we take ourselves out of the place of temptation, we will not yield to temptation as much. We have already made a conscious decision to say no, and we have put ourselves in a place where it is not as easy to sin. (Really now, if getting drunk was a stronghold in your life, would you have a better chance of falling into sin while hanging out in a bar with lost sinners or while praying with friends at a church prayer meeting?)

But we must not only flee from what is bad and destructive. We must pursue what is good and holy. And as much as is possible, we must do it with others who love the Lord, especially in challenging times like this. We are stronger together. We have more resolve together. We are less likely to fall into sin together.

These are just a few strategies to employ if we want to be victors rather than victims at a time when sin is so available and temptation is so pervasive. The devil certainly is tricky, the flesh certainly is powerful, and the world certainly is alluring. But if the Son of God sets us free, and if we live by His teaching rather than being overcome by sin, by His power we will overcome sin. There's no need for you to be a casualty!

CHAPTER 8

WHY SHOULD WE CARE ABOUT WHAT THE BIBLE SAYS?

On June 30, 2022, someone named Robert posted this comment on our ministry's YouTube channel: "Why would anyone in the 21st century give a [expletive] what illiterate desert dwellers from 2000 years ago thought about anything?" In writing this, he reflected the views of many people today, especially in the younger generation. Why on earth should I care about what this old, outmoded, outdated book has to say? What does it have to do with me?

Of course, the authors of the Bible were anything but "illiterate desert dwellers." To this day, scholars are still trying to understand all the nuances of the brilliant Hebrew language found in Job (let alone plumb the philosophical depths of the book), while theologians have written thousands of books and articles debating the meaning of single verses in the writings of Paul. But who cares about facts? It's convenient to bash the Bible and dismiss it out of hand. "I've got better things to do than read the Bible!"

At a point in time in our society, the Bible was widely considered to be the ultimate authority, both morally and legally. A quotation from the Holy Scriptures would end the debate. Not so today. Instead, many Americans, especially younger Americans, look at the Bible with suspicion. According to a 2022 Gallup poll:

> A record-low 20% of Americans now say the Bible is the literal word of God, down from 24% the last time the question was asked in 2017, and half of what it was at its high points in 1980 and 1984. Meanwhile, a new high of 29% say the Bible is a collection of "fables, legends, history and moral precepts recorded by man." This marks the first time significantly more Americans have viewed the Bible as not divinely inspired than as the literal word of God. The largest percentage, 49%, choose the middle alternative, roughly in line with where it has been in previous years.[1]

People are wondering, "Can we really trust what the Bible says? Do we even know what it says? After all, aren't we dealing with translations of translations of translations? Don't the translators have their own sets of biases and presuppositions? And isn't all of this ultimately about power and control? Who says this is the Word of God?"

Rather than dismiss these questions, I want to address them head-on. But I want to do even more than that. I want to give you a fresh perspective on God's Word. I want to invite you to get reacquainted with the most wonderful book that has ever been written. Are you to ready to come along?

In my book *Has God Failed You?*, I devoted two full chapters to the topic "Is the Bible an Outdated and Bigoted Book?" In those chapters, I looked at questions such as: Is the God of the Old Testament cruel? Did the Lord sanction the genocide of the Canaanites? Does God hate LGBTQ+ people? Is the Bible sexist and misogynistic? If those questions interest you, I encourage you to check out the discussion in *Has God Failed You?* Here, we'll address some other critically important questions and issues.

CAN WE TRUST OUR ENGLISH BIBLES?

In recent years I've heard lots of people say that they can't trust any Bibles because they are based on translation upon translation. But the premise of their belief is wrong. Whether you're reading an older English Bible (like the King James Version) or a modern English Bible (like the New International Version, English Standard Version, or New American Standard Bible), you're reading a translation into English straight from biblical Hebrew, biblical Aramaic, or biblical Greek. That's it. You are not reading a translation from Hebrew into Greek into Latin into German into English (or something like that). You are reading a translation straight from the biblical languages (namely, Hebrew and a little Aramaic for the Old Testament and Greek for the New Testament) into English. Everyone who knows anything about Bible translations knows this to be true, and the translators have spent decades studying the original languages and then many years producing their translations. So let's bury that myth about "translations of translations" once and for all.

"But," you say, "I've heard of ancient translations of the Bible like the Septuagint, translating the Hebrew Old Testament into Greek, or the Vulgate, translating the whole Bible into Latin. And then scholars today use those versions, meaning, they use translations of translations. What about that?"

Well, you're right and you're wrong. It is true that such translations exist, dating as far back as 250 years before the time of Jesus. And it is true that scholars use them to see how ancient readers understood the original text. In other words, when a scholar is translating the Hebrew Scriptures into English today, he will see how the Septuagint translated those same verses more than two thousand years ago, seeking to understand the Hebrew as best as possible. Why not use all the tools you have? But then—and this is the key point—that scholar will go directly from the original language into the target language, in this case, English.

"But hang on," you protest. "I understand what you're saying about these scholars going straight from the biblical languages into the modern language they're working with. But you keep talking about 'the original Hebrew' or the 'original Greek,' yet we don't have any original copies of the Bible. We only have copies of copies of copies. So that undermines your whole argument."

Actually, it's true that we only have copies of copies of copies. It's the same with virtually all the major books from the ancient world. But we must remember that the people copying books and verses of the Bible did so with the utmost seriousness, believing these to be sacred texts, even the very Word of God. It's true, of course, that with so much interest in these texts, not every scribe was professionally trained or thoroughly meticulous. But there's good news here too, since we have so many thousands of manuscripts to compare, sorting out the least accurate from the most accurate. The more you dig into this, the more amazing it becomes. That's why when the Dead Sea Scrolls were discovered in the late 1940s, scholars were amazed to see that among the Hebrew manuscripts found there, some of them dating back to as early as 150–100 years BC, some were identical to the text found in our Hebrew Bibles today virtually *letter for letter*.

But this should not surprise us. After all, if you look at a Hebrew Bible today, which is based on manuscripts that are roughly one thousand years old, you'll see a note at the end of the Torah (also known as the Pentateuch, referring to the first five books of the Bible). It lists the total number of verses in the Torah, then the middle verse, then the total number of words in the Torah, then the middle word, then the total number of letters in the Torah—yes, letters. This means that upon finishing his work of copying out the Torah, the scribe would have to go back and count every verse, every word, and every letter. (How many times do you have to count something like that before you're sure you counted correctly?) And what happens if your total deviates by one single letter? You cannot use the manuscript. It is considered defective. Talk about a painstaking job!

And what kind of numbers are we talking about? According to the Hebrew 4 Christians website, there are a total of 5,845 verses in the Hebrew text of the Torah, 79,847 words in the Torah, and 304,805 letters in the Torah. I cannot imagine even trying to count numbers like that accurately, let alone copying out a manuscript to that level of perfection. Little wonder that this same site notes, "There are over 4,000 laws a sofer (scribe) must know before he starts writing the Sefer Torah [Book of the Torah]."[2]

It is true, of course, that these laws and customs post-date the writing of the Old Testament. But they do indicate just how carefully the books of the Bible have been copied and preserved over the centuries. You can be confident that you're reading the same words, even if spelled slightly differently, that previous readers of the Bible read in generations past. Where there are questions about the exact reading of the original text, in the vast majority of cases the variants in question are very minor.

DIGGING DEEPER INTO THE CONTENTS OF THE BIBLE

One of the most common charges against the Bible is that it's just a compilation of ancient myths and stories that were borrowed and tweaked by the biblical writers. In other words, the Bible contains nothing new or inspired. It's just another old book from an old world that was filled with superstitions and fables. Have you heard things like this? Do you believe they might even be true?

Let's take a look at the creation account in Genesis 1, comparing it to one of the most famous ancient Near Eastern creation accounts, called Enuma Elish, written in ancient Babylonian (called Akkadian by scholars). Here are some samples in summarized form from this famous account:

> In the beginning, neither heaven nor earth had names. Apsu, the god of fresh waters, and Tiamat, the goddess of the salt oceans, and Mummu, the god of the mist that rises from both of them, were still mingled as one. There were no mountains, there was no pasture land, and not even a reed-marsh could be found to break the surface of the waters.

It was then that Apsu and Tiamat parented two gods, and then two more who outgrew the first pair. These further parented gods....

Apsu and Tiamat's descendants became an unruly crowd. Eventually Apsu, in his frustration and inability to sleep with the clamor, went to Tiamat, and he proposed to her that he slay their noisy offspring. Tiamat was furious at his suggestion to kill their clan, but after leaving her Apsu resolved to proceed with his murderous plan. When the young gods heard of his plot against them, they were silent and fearful, but soon Ea was hatching a scheme. He cast a spell on Apsu, pulled Apsu's crown from his head, and slew him. Ea then built his palace on Apsu's waters, and it was there that, with the goddess Damkina, he fathered Marduk, the four-eared, four-eyed giant who was god of the rains and storms.

This is pretty wild stuff, but it's just getting started.

The other gods, however, went to Tiamat and complained of how Ea had slain her husband. Aroused, she collected an army of dragons and monsters, and at its head she placed the god Kingu, [to] whom she gave magical powers as well. Even Ea was at a loss how to combat such a host, until he finally called on his son Marduk. Marduk gladly agreed to take on his father's battle, on the condition that he, Marduk, would rule the gods after achieving this victory. The other gods agreed, and at a banquet they gave him his royal robes and scepter.

As the story goes on, "Kingu's battle plan soon disintegrated" in the face of Marduk's attack, and Marduk and

Tiamat were left to battle each other. Tiamat tried to devour Marduk with her mouth, but he unleashed a gale-force wind and an arrow into it. "It split her heart, and she was slain." Afterward, Marduk split her "water-laden body in half like a clam shell. Half he put in the sky and made the heavens, and he posted guards there to make sure that Tiamat's salt waters could not escape...."[3]

So we get heaven and earth from the body of the goddess Tiamat, split in two. Then we have more drama, rebellion, and violence among the gods and their cohorts, which included beings like "the Viper, the Dragon, and the Sphinx, the Great-Lion, the Mad-Dog, and the Scorpion-Man, Mighty lion-demons, the Dragon-Fly, the Centaur."[4]

Contrast this with the opening verses of Genesis 1, and tell me if there is any comparison at all:

> In the beginning God created the heavens and the earth. Now the earth was formless and empty, darkness was over the surface of the deep, and the Spirit of God was hovering over the waters.
>
> And God said, "Let there be light," and there was light. God saw that the light was good, and he separated the light from the darkness. God called the light "day," and the darkness he called "night." And there was evening, and there was morning—the first day.
>
> And God said, "Let there be a vault between the waters to separate water from water." So God made the vault and separated the water under the vault from the water above it. And it was so. God called the vault "sky." And there was evening, and there was morning—the second day.

And God said, "Let the water under the sky be gathered to one place, and let dry ground appear." And it was so. God called the dry ground "land," and the gathered waters he called "seas." And God saw that it was good.

—Genesis 1:1–10

Talk about an extraordinary contrast! Talk about the Bible *not* copying the Babylonian creation account! As I wrote in *Saving a Sick America*:

In stark contrast to these other accounts, the God of Genesis 1 is transcendent and independent: he works systematically and sovereignly, calling light to come out of darkness and order to come out of chaos. By the simple power of his words ("Let there be light!" "Let the earth sprout vegetation!") *something* is brought out of *nothing*, as each command is executed perfectly and without resistance....Genesis 1 is a celebration of life, a celebration of God's triumph over hostile forces, a celebration of his majesty and goodness and wisdom. Ask yourself for a moment: Other than by divine revelation, how would someone gain such an understanding of God in the midst of ancient polytheism? How would a human being conceive of such lofty ideas, not only of a transcendent, independent Lord but of an orderly creation brought about by divine speech?[5]

So at a time when *the whole world was polytheistic and worshipped idols*, the biblical writers were making statements such as, "In the beginning God created the heavens and the earth." Where did they get such lofty ideas? One God and one God only?

Look at what the prophet Isaiah was inspired to write more than twenty-five hundred years ago, again, at a time when in every nation on the planet people bowed down to wooden idols and metal statues of the gods, believing that these images had special power or that they uniquely represented the deities they worshipped. And as you read, ask yourself how the prophets of Israel rose above the superstition and idolatry of the day and saw what others did not see.

> All who make idols are nothing, and the things they treasure are worthless. Those who would speak up for them are blind; they are ignorant, to their own shame.
>
> Who shapes a god and casts an idol, which can profit nothing?
>
> People who do that will be put to shame; such craftsmen are only human beings. Let them all come together and take their stand; they will be brought down to terror and shame.

Then this amazing commentary:

> The blacksmith takes a tool and works with it in the coals; he shapes an idol with hammers, he forges it with the might of his arm. He gets hungry and loses his strength; he drinks no water and grows faint.
>
> The carpenter measures with a line and makes an outline with a marker; he roughs it out with chisels and marks it with compasses. He shapes it in human form, human form in all its glory, that it may dwell in a shrine.
>
> He cut down cedars, or perhaps took a cypress or oak. He let it grow among the trees of the forest, or planted a pine, and the rain made it grow.
>
> It is used as fuel for burning; some of it he takes and

warms himself, he kindles a fire and bakes bread. But he also fashions a god and worships it; he makes an idol and bows down to it.

Half of the wood he burns in the fire; over it he prepares his meal, he roasts his meat and eats his fill. He also warms himself and says, "Ah! I am warm; I see the fire."

From the rest he makes a god, his idol; he bows down to it and worships. He prays to it and says, "Save me! You are my god!"

They know nothing, they understand nothing; their eyes are plastered over so they cannot see, and their minds closed so they cannot understand.

No one stops to think, no one has the knowledge or understanding to say, "Half of it I used for fuel; I even baked bread over its coals, I roasted meat and I ate. Shall I make a detestable thing from what is left? Shall I bow down to a block of wood?"

Such a person feeds on ashes; a deluded heart misleads him; he cannot save himself, or say, "Is not this thing in my right hand a lie?"

Remember these things, Jacob, for you, Israel, are my servant. I have made you, you are my servant; Israel, I will not forget you.

I have swept away your offenses like a cloud, your sins like the morning mist. Return to me, for I have redeemed you.

—Isaiah 44:9–22

Insights like this would be the equivalent of Plato talking about smartphones or Aristotle talking about electric automobiles. That's how foreign these concepts would have sounded to the peoples of the ancient world. Yet to the prophets of

Israel, all this was self-evident. The idols were nothing, and only God was God. So much for the Bible being just like the other books of the ancient world!

And how, exactly, did the God of Israel distinguish Himself from the gods of the nations? He gave them this challenge: "Remember the former things, those of long ago; I am God, and there is no other; I am God, and there is none like me. I make known the end from the beginning, from ancient times, what is still to come. I say, 'My purpose will stand, and I will do all that I please'" (Isa. 46:9–10).

That is exactly what He did, predicting in detail the destruction of the first Temple in Jerusalem in 586 BC, then the exiling of His people to Babylon for seventy years, then their return and the rebuilding of the temple, then the Messiah coming to die and rise while that temple was still standing, then the subsequent destruction of the second temple in 70 AD, then the scattering of the Jewish people around the world, then their great suffering yet still preserved by God, then their return back to their homeland. It's all laid out in advance in the Bible.[6] Show me anything even remotely close to that in any other ancient, or even modern, book.

That's why, around the world to this moment, people are reading from the Bible, quoting the Bible, and looking to the Bible for guidance, wisdom, and inspiration and praying to the God of the Bible rather than praying to Marduk or Baal or reciting passages from ancient hymns to Asherah or Zeus.

WHAT ABOUT BIBLICAL MORALITY?

It is true that we find some Bible verses troubling today, such as the command to drive out (or kill) the Canaanites, a subject I have addressed at length in other books.[7] For the moment, let me just say that there are explanations that make good sense—and I mean good moral sense. But here I want to focus on another subject. What kind of morality does the Bible put forth? How does God call us to live?

Let's start with the Ten Commandments. If you've forgotten them or are not familiar with them, I'll present them here in full:

And God spoke all these words:

"I am the LORD your God, who brought you out of Egypt, out of the land of slavery.

"You shall have no other gods before me.

"You shall not make for yourself an image in the form of anything in heaven above or on the earth beneath or in the waters below. You shall not bow down to them or worship them; for I, the LORD your God, am a jealous God, punishing the children for the sin of the parents to the third and fourth generation of those who hate me, but showing love to a thousand generations of those who love me and keep my commandments.

"You shall not misuse the name of the LORD your God, for the LORD will not hold anyone guiltless who misuses his name.

"Remember the Sabbath day by keeping it holy. Six days you shall labor and do all your work, but the seventh day is a sabbath to the LORD your God. On it you shall not do any work, neither you, nor your son or daughter, nor your male or female servant, nor your animals, nor any foreigner residing in your towns. For in six days the LORD made the heavens and the earth, the sea, and all that is in them, but he rested on the seventh day. Therefore the LORD blessed the Sabbath day and made it holy.

> "Honor your father and your mother, so that you may live long in the land the LORD your God is giving you.
>
> "You shall not murder.
>
> "You shall not commit adultery.
>
> "You shall not steal.
>
> "You shall not give false testimony against your neighbor.
>
> "You shall not covet your neighbor's house. You shall not covet your neighbor's wife, or his male or female servant, his ox or donkey, or anything that belongs to your neighbor."
>
> —EXODUS 20:1–17

Now, ask yourself this question: If the whole world lived by these words, would the world be a better place? A safer place? A healthier place? A more moral place? Would it be easier for you to raise your kids in an environment like this? Would there be less crime? Would marriages be stronger? Would people be more at peace with themselves and one another? The answer is obviously yes—unless you think that more murder, more adultery, more theft, more lying, more dishonoring of parents, more covetousness, more workaholism, and more worship of false gods would make the world a better place. Yet these Ten Commandments lay the moral foundation of the rest of the Old Testament. Perhaps the Bible has some divine wisdom after all.

That's why the pages of the Old Testament are filled with calls to justice, like these:

> Seek good, not evil, that you may live. Then the LORD God Almighty will be with you, just as you say he is. Hate evil, love good; maintain justice in the courts.
>
> —AMOS 5:14–15

> Wash and make yourselves clean. Take your evil deeds out of my sight; stop doing wrong. Learn to do right; seek justice. Defend the oppressed. Take up the cause of the fatherless; plead the case of the widow
>
> —Isaiah 1:16–17

> [Speaking of a godly king in Judah]: "He did what was right and just, so all went well with him. He defended the cause of the poor and needy, and so all went well. Is that not what it means to know me?" declares the Lord.
>
> —Jeremiah 22:15–16

So knowing God and being in right relationship with Him is demonstrated by caring for the poor and needy. That's in the Bible too!

That's why God, speaking through His prophets, made clear that He despised the religious hypocrisy of His people, as they filled the temple with songs of praises while living like the devil when they left the temple courts. As the Lord said through Amos, "I hate, I despise your religious festivals; your assemblies are a stench to me. Even though you bring me burnt offerings and grain offerings, I will not accept them. Though you bring choice fellowship offerings, I will have no regard for them. Away with the noise of your songs! I will not listen to the music of your harps. But let justice roll on like a river, righteousness like a never-failing stream" (Amos 5:21–24)!

Did you know verses like this were in the Bible? There are actually quite a few just like this. To repeat: the Lord hates religious hypocrisy, right until this day.

How about the moral standards of Jesus? Try these on for a fit (and note the Lord's use of hyperbole to drive home His point):

> You have heard that it was said, "You shall not commit
> adultery." But I tell you that anyone who looks at a woman
> lustfully has already committed adultery with her in his
> heart. If your right eye causes you to stumble, gouge it
> out and throw it away. It is better for you to lose one part
> of your body than for your whole body to be thrown into
> hell. And if your right hand causes you to stumble, cut it
> off and throw it away. It is better for you to lose one part
> of your body than for your whole body to go into hell.
>
> —MATTHEW 5:27–30

So outward holiness is not the only thing that matters.
God is looking at our hearts. Ouch!

And to those "who were confident of their own righteousness and looked down on everyone else," Jesus gave the following parable. (For background, the Pharisees were highly
respected religious leaders; tax collectors were infamous for
their corruption.)

> Two men went up to the temple to pray, one a Pharisee
> and the other a tax collector. The Pharisee stood by
> himself and prayed: "God, I thank you that I am not like
> other people—robbers, evildoers, adulterers—or even
> like this tax collector. I fast twice a week and give a
> tenth of all I get."
>
> But the tax collector stood at a distance. He would
> not even look up to heaven, but beat his breast and said,
> "God, have mercy on me, a sinner."
>
> I tell you that this man, rather than the other, went
> home justified before God. For all those who exalt them-
> selves will be humbled, and those who humble them-
> selves will be exalted.
>
> —LUKE 18:10–14

You can see why so many of the common people loved Jesus and why so many of the religious leaders hated Him.

Jesus also stood with the outcast and the marginalized, challenging racial injustice and prejudice. In fact, that's the subject of one of His most famous teachings, the parable of the good Samaritan. For background here, the Samaritans were considered half-breeds by the larger Jewish community, viewed as the descendants of a mixture of pagans and Israelites. They were, at best, second-class citizens. And Jesus gave this teaching when interacting with a religious scholar about the command to "love your neighbor as yourself." The scholar, wanting to exempt himself from loving people he didn't consider his neighbor—such as his enemies or simply people he didn't like—asked, "And who is my neighbor?" Jesus replied:

> "A man was going down from Jerusalem to Jericho, when he was attacked by robbers. They stripped him of his clothes, beat him and went away, leaving him half dead. A priest happened to be going down the same road, and when he saw the man, he passed by on the other side. So too, a Levite, when he came to the place and saw him, passed by on the other side. But a Samaritan, as he traveled, came where the man was; and when he saw him, he took pity on him. He went to him and bandaged his wounds, pouring on oil and wine. Then he put the man on his own donkey, brought him to an inn and took care of him. The next day he took out two denarii and gave them to the innkeeper. 'Look after him,' he said, 'and when I return, I will reimburse you for any extra expense you may have.'
>
> "Which of these three do you think was a neighbor to the man who fell into the hands of robbers?"

> The expert in the law replied, "The one who had mercy on him." Jesus told him, "Go and do likewise."
>
> —Luke 10:30–37

To say it again, ouch! Talk about undercutting our self-righteousness. Talk about turning the tables. Talk about painting the picture of an unexpected hero—the Samaritan—in contrast with the religious leaders who, quite literally, didn't want to get their hands dirty. Talk about putting the responsibility on us to be loving neighbors.

This is the Jesus we love and celebrate. This is the world changer we follow. This is the one we seek to emulate. Are you starting to see why?

IS THERE ROOM FOR YOUR QUESTIONS?

Some of you might say, "Look, I do love Jesus, and I do find great value in the Bible. But I have so many doubts and questions, and I feel I can't relate to people who are full of faith and never seem to question anything. That's just not me."

Well, I have good news for you too. God saw you coming. He knew there would be people just like you. That's why He used some of them to write parts of the Bible! He includes the prayers of people who felt forsaken by God. He includes words of challenge, where people in great suffering accused God of being unfair—and even worse (just read the Book of Job!). He includes words of skepticism, taking you on a journey with these biblical authors who expressed their cynical attitudes.

Foremost among these is Ecclesiastes (in Hebrew, Koheleth), which means the teacher or the gatherer (perhaps, of sayings) or the convener. And he writes and speaks in the name and spirit of King Solomon of old. This is how the book starts:

"Meaningless! Meaningless!" says the Teacher. "Utterly meaningless! Everything is meaningless."

What do people gain from all their labors at which they toil under the sun? Generations come and generations go, but the earth remains forever. The sun rises and the sun sets, and hurries back to where it rises.

The wind blows to the south and turns to the north; round and round it goes, ever returning on its course. All streams flow into the sea, yet the sea is never full. To the place the streams come from, there they return again. All things are wearisome, more than one can say. The eye never has enough of seeing, nor the ear its fill of hearing.

What has been will be again, what has been done will be done again; there is nothing new under the sun. Is there anything of which one can say, "Look! This is something new"? It was here already, long ago; it was here before our time.

No one remembers the former generations, and even those yet to come will not be remembered by those who follow them.

—ECCLESIASTES 1:2–11

Have you ever felt this way? Remember, what you just read is part of the Bible! And this:

Everyone's toil is for their mouth, yet their appetite is never satisfied.

What advantage have the wise over fools? What do the poor gain by knowing how to conduct themselves before others?

Better what the eye sees than the roving of the appetite. This too is meaningless, a chasing after the wind.

Whatever exists has already been named, and what humanity is has been known; no one can contend with someone who is stronger.

The more the words, the less the meaning, and how does that profit anyone?

For who knows what is good for a person in life, during the few and meaningless days they pass through like a shadow? Who can tell them what will happen under the sun after they are gone?

—ECCLESIASTES 6:7–12

And this:

I have seen something else under the sun: The race is not to the swift or the battle to the strong, nor does food come to the wise or wealth to the brilliant or favor to the learned; but time and chance happen to them all.

Moreover, no one knows when their hour will come: As fish are caught in a cruel net, or birds are taken in a snare, so people are trapped by evil times that fall unexpectedly upon them.

—ECCLESIASTES 9:11–12

Yet in the end, having examined the meaning (and apparent meaninglessness) of life, this teacher ended his book with these sobering words: "Now all has been heard; here is the conclusion of the matter: Fear God and keep his commandments, for this is the duty of all mankind. For God will bring every deed into judgment, including every hidden thing, whether it is good or evil" (Eccles. 12:13–14). His skepticism and cynicism ran their course, finding eloquent expression in the twelve chapters of this book called Ecclesiastes. But in the end, there was only one conclusion: everything comes down to our relationship with God and our obedience to His commandments.

There's a verse in Jude that calls on believers to "be merciful to those who doubt" (Jude 22). I wrote a whole chapter on this titled "Permission to Doubt" in *Has God Failed You?* Suffice it to say that God understands your skepticism, questions, and doubts, and if you are sincere (rather than arrogant or mocking), He will meet you where you are and help you get where you need to be: a place of solid, unshakable, wonderfully rich and rewarding faith.

THE BIBLE IS OH SO PRACTICAL TOO

We all know that there are incredible, inspirational passages in the Bible, passages that have stood the test of time. Just think of these words written by King David about three thousand years ago, a time known as the Iron Age. (Yes, that *was* a long time ago.) David was a shepherd as a boy, so he was the perfect one to pen these words. Aren't they still beautiful and inspiring all these centuries later?

> The LORD is my shepherd, I lack nothing. He makes me lie down in green pastures, he leads me beside quiet waters, he refreshes my soul. He guides me along the right paths for his name's sake. Even though I walk through the darkest valley, I will fear no evil, for you are with me; your rod and your staff, they comfort me. You prepare a table before me in the presence of my enemies. You anoint my head with oil; my cup overflows. Surely your goodness and love will follow me all the days of my life, and I will dwell in the house of the LORD forever.
>
> —PSALM 23:1–6

Many a time, in the midst of the storms of life, I have taken hold of these words, reciting them by memory in Hebrew, and they have brought peace to my soul.

Or has anyone ever, at any time or in any place, penned a more beautiful and succinct description of love? This is what Paul wrote almost two thousand years ago:

> If I speak in the tongues of men or of angels, but do not have love, I am only a resounding gong or a clanging cymbal. If I have the gift of prophecy and can fathom all mysteries and all knowledge, and if I have a faith that can move mountains, but do not have love, I am nothing. If I give all I possess to the poor and give over my body to hardship that I may boast, but do not have love, I gain nothing.
>
> Love is patient, love is kind. It does not envy, it does not boast, it is not proud. It does not dishonor others, it is not self-seeking, it is not easily angered, it keeps no record of wrongs. Love does not delight in evil but rejoices with the truth. It always protects, always trusts, always hopes, always perseveres.
>
> Love never fails. But where there are prophecies, they will cease; where there are tongues, they will be stilled; where there is knowledge, it will pass away. For we know in part and we prophesy in part, but when completeness comes, what is in part disappears. When I was a child, I talked like a child, I thought like a child, I reasoned like a child. When I became a man, I put the ways of childhood behind me. For now we see only a reflection as in a mirror; then we shall see face to face. Now I know in part; then I shall know fully, even as I am fully known. And now these three remain: faith, hope and love. But the greatest of these is love.
>
> —1 Corinthians 13:1–13

What an ode to love!

But the Bible is practical too, telling us what love looks like in action: "This is how we know what love is: Jesus Christ laid down his life for us. And we ought to lay down our lives for our brothers and sisters. If anyone has material possessions and sees a brother or sister in need but has no pity on them, how can the love of God be in that person? Dear children, let us not love with words or speech but with actions and in truth" (1 John 3:16–18).

The Bible also offers wise, down-to-earth counsel like this: "When you sit to dine with a ruler, note well what is before you, and put a knife to your throat if you are given to gluttony. Do not crave his delicacies, for that food is deceptive" (Prov. 23:1–3). And this: "Go to the ant, you sluggard; consider its ways and be wise! It has no commander, no overseer or ruler, yet it stores its provisions in summer and gathers its food at harvest. How long will you lie there, you sluggard? When will you get up from your sleep? A little sleep, a little slumber, a little folding of the hands to rest—and poverty will come on you like a thief and scarcity like an armed man" (Prov. 6:6–11).

How about this description of the folly of getting drunk over and over again?

> Who has woe? Who has sorrow? Who has strife? Who has complaints? Who has needless bruises? Who has bloodshot eyes? Those who linger over wine, who go to sample bowls of mixed wine.
>
> Do not gaze at wine when it is red, when it sparkles in the cup, when it goes down smoothly! In the end it bites like a snake and poisons like a viper.
>
> Your eyes will see strange sights, and your mind will imagine confusing things. You will be like one sleeping

on the high seas, lying on top of the rigging. "They hit me," you will say, "but I'm not hurt! They beat me, but I don't feel it! When will I wake up so I can find another drink?"

—PROVERBS 23:29–35

The Bible also contains powerful descriptions of the seduction of sexual sin (read through Proverbs 7 when you have time; talk about nailing it) and the destructive power of the tongue. (Check out Jacob [James] 3 for this.) And there are beautiful pictures of the end of the age when God's kingdom will fill the earth:

> The wolf will live with the lamb, the leopard will lie down with the goat, the calf and the lion and the yearling together; and a little child will lead them. The cow will feed with the bear, their young will lie down together, and the lion will eat straw like the ox. The infant will play near the cobra's den, and the young child will put its hand into the viper's nest. They will neither harm nor destroy on all my holy mountain, for the earth will be filled with the knowledge of the LORD as the waters cover the sea.
>
> —ISAIAH 11:6–9

This will be the answer to the prayer that Jesus taught His followers to pray, saying, "Our Father in heaven, hallowed be your name, your kingdom come, your will be done, on earth as it is in heaven" (Matt. 6:9–10). And in the end, for those who love the Lord, "They will be his people, and God himself will be with them and be their God. 'He will wipe every tear from their eyes. There will be no more death' or mourning or crying or pain, for the old order of things has passed away"

(Rev. 21:3–4). This is what we look forward to in the midst of this fallen and broken world.

These are just some of the amazing treasures found in the Word of God. I haven't even touched on the many revolutionary statements found in the Bible, like Paul's words that, in Jesus, "there is neither Jew nor Gentile, neither slave nor free, nor is there male and female, for you are all one in Christ Jesus" (Gal. 3:28). Of course, he recognized differences between men and women, and he knew that Jews and Gentiles were distinct and that there was such a thing as the slavery system. But he was emphasizing that, as children of God by faith, we are all equal and there is no caste system and no class system, one of the most radical, revolutionary statements made in religious history. Little wonder, then, that where the true Christian message has spread, it has liberated women from oppression, called on men to live morally, and over time abolished the slave trade and the slave system.

May I urge you not to get hung up on a few difficult verses or passages and instead to dive in and drink deeply of the life-giving waters of the Word of God? Read through the Gospels if you never have. Read through Proverbs and Psalms. Even check out Genesis, and start in the beginning. And pray this prayer before you read: "Open my eyes, that I may see wonderful things in Your Teaching" (Ps. 119:18, my translation). You will never be the same.

CHAPTER 9

HOW COULD A GOOD GOD SEND BILLIONS OF PEOPLE TO HELL?

As the world gets smaller and smaller, it has become increasingly difficult to think of people we don't know as "they" or "them"—meaning nameless, faceless people who are so different from us that we have no sympathy or concern for them. Today "they" are our friends on social media, even if they live in a small village in Africa. "They" are real people with families like ours and with feelings like ours. "They" are fellow human beings, and their tragedies and joys are now our tragedies and joys as we watch their lives unfold on our cell phones in real time. It doesn't seem so easy to say today, "Well, if 'they' don't believe in Jesus, 'they' are all going to hell."

Is it really that simple? Is God that narrow? What about all those who never heard about Jesus? What about those who learned about another God, like the nearly two billion

Muslims or the roughly fifteen million Jews? What about the devout Hindus and the practicing Buddhists? What about the kindhearted atheists? Do any of them, let alone all of them, deserve to go to hell forever?

Since the real question is, "What does the Bible say about hell and eternal judgment?," we should let the Bible speak for itself. After all, the issue is not what Dante's *Inferno* says about future punishment, nor is it what your church or my church teaches. Instead, what matters is what the Bible actually says about hell, judgment, and future punishment. Can we take a few minutes to examine it together? You might be surprised with what we discover.

Let's start with an even bigger question: What is the God of the Bible like? Does He simply create billions of people to destroy them? Does He delight in wiping out the world with floods and disasters? Will He sit in heaven gleefully torturing the work of His hands—human beings!—for ever and ever? When I heard from many atheists in July 2022 in response to a series of questions I had posted, they were almost totally unanimous in saying, "If the God of the Bible really existed, I would not follow Him." In their eyes, He was a moral monster. What, then, does the Bible really say about this God?

It is true that, in the Bible, He poured out devastating judgments, including the flood in Noah's day.[1] In fact, I could fill much of this book with quotations of long biblical passages describing—or threatening—those very judgments. And it is true that the Bible speaks of final, irreversible judgments that He will bring. But it also says that He *longs* to show mercy and that He *prefers* to show mercy. In fact, according to the Scriptures, *the Lord will look for every opportunity to show mercy before He pours out judgment*. Here are some verses describing the attitude of God when it comes to sending judgment:

- This was spoken by the prophet Isaiah when Israel continued to rebel and reject God's warnings: "Yet the LORD longs to be gracious to you; therefore he will rise up to show you compassion. For the LORD is a God of justice. Blessed are all who wait for him" (Isa. 30:18)! God longs to be gracious to His people!

- This was spoken by the prophet Micah during a similar period of time: "Who is a God like you, who pardons sin and forgives the transgression of the remnant of his inheritance? You do not stay angry forever but delight to show mercy. You will again have compassion on us; you will tread our sins underfoot and hurl all our iniquities into the depths of the sea. You will be faithful to Jacob, and show love to Abraham, as you pledged on oath to our ancestors in days long ago" (Mic. 7:18–20). The Lord doesn't hold on to His anger forever but delights to show mercy!

- Consider what David said about the Lord in Psalms: "The LORD is compassionate and gracious, slow to anger, abounding in love. He will not always accuse, nor will he harbor his anger forever; he does not treat us as our sins deserve or repay us according to our iniquities. For as high as the heavens are above the earth, so great is his love for those who fear him; as far as the east is from the west, so far has he removed our transgressions from us. As a father has compassion on his children, so the LORD has compassion on those who fear him; for he knows how we are formed, he remembers that we are dust" (Ps. 103:8–14). Could you imagine a more loving, patient, and caring description of God than this?

- This is what He said through the prophet Ezekiel when the people of Judah were in exile because of their sins: "Rid yourselves of all the offenses you have committed, and get a new heart and a new spirit. Why will you die, people of Israel? For I take no pleasure in the death of anyone, declares the Sovereign LORD. Repent and live" (Ezek. 18:31–32)! God wants us to do what is right so He can forgive. He takes no delight in punishing a wicked person.[2]

- He even expressed this desire through the prophet Isaiah: "This is what the LORD says— your Redeemer, the Holy One of Israel: 'I am the LORD your God, who teaches you what is best for you, who directs you in the way you should go. If only you had paid attention to my commands, your peace would have been like a river, your well-being like the waves of the sea. Your descendants would have been like the sand, your children like its numberless grains; their name would never be blotted out nor destroyed from before

me'" (Isa. 48:17–19). He will not force us to do
what is right and best, but He really wants us to.

- And this is what Jesus Himself said to the people
  and leaders of Jerusalem: "Jerusalem, Jerusalem,
  you who kill the prophets and stone those sent to
  you, how often I have longed to gather your children together, as a hen gathers her chicks under
  her wings, and you were not willing" (Matt.
  23:37–38). Our Savior was saying, "I have been
  wanting to take care of you and do good things
  for you for so long, but you were not willing."

Perhaps this is a different picture of the Lord than you
have seen? Perhaps the caricatured attacks on the God of the
Bible bear little resemblance to who He really is? To repeat:
it is true that God has poured out His judgments throughout
history and that He will do so again in the future. But it is
only because that is the right and just thing to do. He is not
cavalier. He is not short-tempered. He does not have bad days.
And He is not a sadist.

Just like a judge who passes a just sentence on a serial rapist
and murderer—it would be a crime to give him five years in
prison or simply put him on parole—our God does what is
just and right. But even then, He gives us ample opportunity to turn from our evil deeds and turn back to Him. As
the verses we just cited make clear, He is slow to anger and
great in mercy, not slow to mercy and great in anger. He
understands human weakness. He loves to find a reason to
forgive. In the words of John, "God is love" (1 John 4:8)—not
hate, not anger, not meanness, not pettiness. No, God, in

His very essence and to the core of His being, is love. As John wrote:

> Dear friends, let us love one another, for love comes from God. Everyone who loves has been born of God and knows God. Whoever does not love does not know God, because God is love. This is how God showed his love among us: He sent his one and only Son into the world that we might live through him. This is love: not that we loved God, but that he loved us and sent his Son as an atoning sacrifice for our sins. Dear friends, since God so loved us, we also ought to love one another. No one has ever seen God; but if we love one another, God lives in us and his love is made complete in us.
>
> —1 JOHN 4:7–12

Yes, this is in the Bible too!

And when Moses really wanted to know and understand the Lord better, He revealed His very nature to him, saying this of Himself:

> Yahweh! The LORD! The God of compassion and mercy! I am slow to anger and filled with unfailing love and faithfulness. I lavish unfailing love to a thousand generations. I forgive iniquity, rebellion, and sin. But I do not excuse the guilty. I lay the sins of the parents upon their children and grandchildren; the entire family is affected— even children in the third and fourth generations.
>
> —EXODUS 34:6–7, NLT

Can you raise a moral objection to this description of God? Can you see how His mercy far outweighs His judgment, as He shows His love for a thousand generations but

His punishment for three or four generations?[3] And who is it that He punishes? The guilty. The ones who refuse to repent. Those who spurn His commandments, along with their children who follow in their footsteps. And what happens to those children or grandchildren who turn to Him for mercy and change their ways? He pours out His love on them.

But the Bible doesn't stop there. Instead, all of the Bible moves toward one central point, the place where the fullness of God's love and mercy and long-suffering are poured out—the cross! It is there that the Lord makes the ultimate statement of His goodness, declaring in essence to a sinning, rebelling world, "No matter what you have done and no matter how evil you are—that includes terrorists and torturers, rapists and rebels, perverts and pimps, drug dealers and drunkards—My Son has paid for your sins, every single one of them. And if you turn to Me for mercy and turn away from your sins, putting your trust in Jesus, He will take away your sins—all of them! And rather than cast you into hell, I will forgive you and cleanse you and give you a new heart and take you into My family, and we will live together forever."

Can you look me in the eye and tell me that is not the most mind-blowing expression of mercy imaginable? Can you tell me that God is not going far beyond anything we could have possibly asked for? His Son dying for what we did? We blew it, and He paid for it? We were guilty, and He suffered? The perfect Son of God came into our world and was rejected, mocked, beaten, and crucified because we were so rotten? And when we look to Him for mercy and forgiveness and new life, we receive the reward for His perfection? How can this be? Talk about grace and unmerited favor beyond limit, imagination, or comprehension. But this is who our

God is, and this is the central theme of the Bible. So much for the cavalier madman roasting sinners in eternal fire and laughing with glee as He tortures us. Perish the very thought.

Please take a few minutes to chew on this and digest what you have read. There's a lot to unpack here, a lot that is contrary to how we think about God. In fact, through the prophet Jeremiah He explained that, even when He is bringing judgment on His disobedient people, His heart still longs for them: "'Is not Ephraim my dear son, the child in whom I delight? Though I often speak against him, I still remember him. Therefore my heart yearns for him; I have great compassion for him,' declares the LORD" (Jer. 31:20). That is the God of the Bible. There is even a verse that declares that "judgment without mercy will be shown to anyone who has not been merciful. Mercy triumphs over judgment" (Jas. 2:13).

A STUDY IN CONTRASTS

Now compare God's goodness to our badness. We hate one another. We steal from one another. We murder one another. We commit adultery. We go to war and commit atrocities against one another. (So much senseless and needless bloodshed!) We lie, deceive, and cheat. We are full of pride, greed, and lust. We are self-righteous. We are hypocrites. The list is really endless. Just look at our conduct on social media. We are vicious, heartless, and nasty. We bully, embarrass, and humiliate. We are harsh, judgmental, and impatient. This is a picture of the human heart!

You might say, "I've never murdered anyone. Or committed adultery. Or even stolen. I'm actually a pretty good person."

Perhaps you are—when compared to other human beings. But may I ask you honestly, How many times have you lied or deceived? How many lustful thoughts have you had or lustful acts have you committed? How many times have you judged others harshly, in fact, judging them in the exact opposite way that you want to be judged? How many times have you acted selfishly? How often have you failed to love your neighbor as yourself? How many times have you been filled with pride?

I was having lunch with a colleague in Holland, eating the same meal I had eaten hundreds of times: a giant, super-healthy salad with a low-fat, low-sodium dressing, in this case, lite balsamic vinaigrette. As always, I shook the closed bottle, then I poured the dressing over the salad, tossed the salad, and began to eat. But this time something was different. All over the table there were little drops of that dark brown dressing—and I mean lots of them. What happened? Well, we were sitting at an all-white table—a very white table—and against that backdrop, all the droplets showed up.

Suddenly I realized that most likely every single day, when I prepared and ate my large salad, I was making a minor mess, as the salad dressing sprayed out over the bowl and onto the table, especially when I tossed the salad. It's just that the tables (or tablecloths) where I normally ate, at home or on the road, had some color to them. That's why I couldn't see the mess.

It's the same with us and our sin. We don't realize how dark or ugly our sins are until we hold them up in the light of God's goodness and perfection. Suddenly, we realize that we really deserve judgment, that we cannot boast about our righteousness and goodness, that we really do need mercy—every single one of us. In fact, the more we pursue God and seek to please Him, the more we become aware of our own shortcomings, failings, and guilt.

It is true that we, as human beings, have many wonderful

qualities. That's because we are made in God's image, and on some level we reflect His morality and goodness. At the same time, we really are a fallen race. That's why, as I write these words, somewhere in this world men are getting aroused by watching infants and toddlers being sexually abused. (By day, these men are successful and respected businessmen in their communities. No one would imagine the perversion of their secret lives.) Someone else has just kidnapped a teenage girl who will soon be trafficked as a sex slave. (These traffickers have so dehumanized their victims that they see them simply as commodities to be bought and sold. They can make a good living off their victims.) A woman lives in luxury with her husband who became rich by selling fentanyl. (It doesn't trouble her that innocent people died of overdoses to support her lifestyle.) A father beats his wife and children, scarring them physically and emotionally for life. (But this is what he watched his own father do. What else should we expect?)

Once again, the list goes on and on. This too is a picture of the human race. And if anything, the big question we should ask is this: Why is God waiting so long to take action? If it were up to some of us, we would start wiping all these people out. It turns out that the Lord is a lot more long-suffering than we are.

And what of the casualties of war? Speaking of World War II alone, Jennifer Rosenberg wrote that it ranks as the "largest and bloodiest war" "of all time" and that it "involved most of the planet." She noted that "between 62 and 78 million are estimated to have died" and that "the huge majority (over 50 million) were civilians."[4] Yet not a single one of these deaths was necessary. They were all caused by human pride, ambition, and cruelty.

Some scholars have claimed that Communism in the twentieth century was responsible for the death of one hundred million people, a number that is disputed by other scholars.[5] But on any count, tens of millions of people died for no good reason at all. Welcome to the human race. And at this very moment, America and Russia own thousands of nuclear warheads (at one point in time, we had tens of thousands of such weapons).[6] The United States' most powerful of these warheads is the B83, "which has a maximum yield of 1.2 megatons, making it 60 times more powerful than the bomb dropped on Nagasaki, Japan, in 1945. According to the Nuclear Weapon Archive, 650 B83s are in 'active service.'"[7]

And why, pray tell, do we spend so much money—billions upon billions of dollars—on these massively destructive, potentially world-ending bombs? Because we know that if we don't, the bad guys (be it Russia or China or some terrorist-supporting nation) might use their weapons on us. If we're not ready to kill more of them more quickly than they can kill us, we're not safe. What a picture of our fallen state!

It would be like an arms race between two distrusting neighbors. You see your neighbor bring home a small knife, so you buy a bigger knife. He sees you bring that home, so he buys a handgun, so you buy a rifle, so he buys an AR15, so you buy a machine gun, so he buys a bazooka...As crazy as this sounds, this is how the nations of the world conduct themselves, spending countless billions of dollars in the process—meaning countless billions of dollars that could have been used for practical, humanitarian causes. Instead, we spend it to stockpile weapons.

And what would we do as human beings if we weren't afraid of getting caught and if there were no immediate consequences for our sins? How much more adultery would there be? How much more stealing? How much more evil? Isn't this why the moment a major power outage occurs, people start looting stores? No one will catch us in the dark! And can you imagine what our society would look like without courts, jails, and prisons? Do you really, truly think that we are not deserving of judgment as a race?

You might say, "Fair enough. But we didn't ask to be put here. We didn't ask to have free will. That's on God, not on us."

So would you prefer that you—and the rest of the human race—never existed? Would you prefer that God never created us? For the vast majority of us, our answer would be, "No. We're glad we have the opportunity to live." That's why so few of us take our own lives. Life is the most precious thing we have.

What about our free wills? What if I told you, "Doctors can perform surgery on your brain that will remove your ability to make bad choices. But you will be very happy." Would you say, "Sign me up for that surgery"? I seriously doubt it. Next to our very lives, the thing we prize most is our freedom of choice. But with life and freedom come consequences, and one day we will give account to our Creator. How did we handle the gifts of life and freedom of choice?

On that day there will be two possible outcomes: We will receive mercy, forgiveness, and grace through the cross, getting the opposite of what we deserve. Or we will receive exactly what we deserve. What is so wrong with that? Why should we protest that outcome? What is unfair or unjust about it? God will treat us fairly.

Here's what Paul wrote in Romans:

God "will repay each person according to what they have done." To those who by persistence in doing good seek glory, honor and immortality, he will give eternal life. But for those who are self-seeking and who reject the truth and follow evil, there will be wrath and anger. There will be trouble and distress for every human being who does evil: first for the Jew, then for the Gentile; but glory, honor and peace for everyone who does good: first for the Jew, then for the Gentile. For God does not show favoritism.
—ROMANS 2:6–11, WITH PAUL QUOTING PSALM 62:12

If you are good enough to merit eternal life, you will receive it. If you deserve wrath and anger, you will receive it. The question is: Are any of us good enough, in and of ourselves, to merit eternal life? For my part, I'll take the mercy option. "God, don't judge me by what I deserve, but judge me based on Your grace and mercy through Jesus!"

You might say, "Even if what you're saying is true, what happens to all the people who never heard about Jesus? And what about devout people in other religions whose version of Jesus is different from yours? What happens to them?"

Those are all great questions. The Bible does not have a specific verse that says, "This is how God will judge those who never heard the gospel." The Bible *does* say that all human beings are without excuse before God. (See Romans 1:17–32.) But it also says, "How, then, can they call on the one they have not believed in? And how can they believe in the one of whom they have not heard? And how can they hear without someone preaching to them? And how can anyone preach unless they are sent? As it is written: 'How beautiful are the feet of those who bring good news'" (Rom. 10:14–15)! That's why missionaries take Jesus' message around the world so that everyone can hear. That's why Christians share their faith with others. They want everyone to have an opportunity to receive forgiveness, mercy, and new life.

Still, we recognize that even now there are multiplied hundreds of millions of people who have never heard the gospel. In fact, if you asked them if they know Jesus, they might think you're talking about someone in their village—or maybe even about the name of another village. "Jesus? Who is that? Or where is that?"

And there are tens of thousands of ultra-Orthodox Jews who believe Jesus was an evil man, a deceiver and idol worshipper who led Israel astray, the founder of a terrible religion called Christianity, which has persecuted the Jewish people throughout history and which ultimately led to the Holocaust. Yet these same Jews pray daily to the God of Abraham, Isaac, and Jacob and seek to be loyal to their God no matter what, observing the Torah and their traditions. What happens to them? With all their sincerity and devotion, do they burn in hell forever?

I could give you all kinds of theoretical answers, delving deeply into philosophy and theology, sounding sophisticated and deep, but instead I will simply say this: *God will treat them fairly*. God will do what is right. God will act in accordance with His nature. That is enough to satisfy me, and if you believe that the Lord we worship is perfect in justice and perfect in mercy, then that should satisfy you too.

But more relevant right now is that *you* have heard about Jesus. You have heard the message of forgiveness through the cross. You have heard that the Savior paid for your sins. If you reject Him, you do it with your eyes wide open. Is God to blame for that? And if you're struggling in your faith and not sure who or what you can believe, I urge you to keep your heart soft before God, telling Him, "If You're really there and the Bible is really true, I want to believe. Help my unbelief."[8]

BUT WHAT ABOUT HELL?

At this point, you might feel that *some* of your questions have been answered. I certainly hope that is the case. Still, the biggest question of all is the one we have not tackled yet. What about hell? What about eternal punishment? What about people burning forever in the lake of fire? What about verses like Daniel 12:2? It states, "Multitudes who sleep in the dust of the earth will awake: some to everlasting life, others to shame and everlasting contempt." What about the words of Jesus in Matthew 25:46? He said, "Then they [the wicked] will go away to eternal punishment, but the righteous to eternal life." What about Revelation 20:15? "Anyone whose name was not found written in the book of life was thrown into the lake of fire." And what about Revelation 14:11? It declares, "And the smoke of their torment will rise for ever and ever."

Some would argue that people will not burn in fire forever. Instead, the images of fire and smoke are figures of speech representing acute suffering and pain. Still, it's not very comforting to say, "Well, you won't burn in fire forever, but you will suffer acutely forever." That still sounds incredibly harsh for the sins we commit in this life. Where is the justice in that?

In response, it could be argued that we have sinned against an eternal God, and therefore our punishment should be eternal. But what if someone had no idea they were sinning against this eternal being? What if they really thought they were doing good and helping others? What if they were trying to be faithful to the religious tradition in which they were raised? How is such a sentence fair?

Some would say, "But that's the thing. Deep down, people really are in rebellion against God, and on that day of accounting, rather than pleading for mercy, they will shake their fists at God. And when He pronounces judgment on them, rather than saying, 'I accept Your judgment as just,' they will blaspheme Him and revile Him. And they will keep doing this forever; that's why their punishment lasts forever." If that is an accurate description, then, to repeat, people will simply get what they deserve.

Others, however, would say that we're missing the whole point of eternal punishment, arguing that over time, as we are separated from God and under judgment, we will degenerate to the point that we are hardly even conscious. The fires, so to say, will keep burning, but we will simply fade away into oblivion.

C. S. Lewis, considered by many to be the most influential Christian apologist of the twentieth century, addressed the question of hell head-on. He wrote, "There is no doctrine which I would more willingly remove from Christianity than this, if it lay in my power. But it has the full support of Scripture and, specially, of Our Lord's own words; it has always been held by Christendom; and it has the support of reason. If a game is played, it must be possible to lose it."[9]

He also wrote, "I willingly believe that the damned are, in one sense, successful, rebels to the end; that the doors of hell are locked on the *inside*."[10] So people, to their dying breath and then forever afterward, will reject God and want no part of an eternal, holy heaven. When they say to God, "Get away from me," He will say, "So be it."

But Lewis made a further observation about the state of those who ultimately reject their Creator:

> To enter heaven is to become more human than you ever succeeded in being on earth; to enter hell is to be banished from humanity. What is cast (or casts itself) into hell is not a man: it is "remains." To be a complete man means to have the passions obedient to the will and the will offered to God: to *have been* a man—to be an ex-man or "damned ghost"—would presumably mean to consist of a will utterly centered in its self and passions utterly uncontrolled by the will.[11]

There are others, however, who take things one step further. They fully acknowledge that there are eternal, dreadful consequences for rejecting God's mercy. They recognize that a real hell with real fire exists. And they believe that future judgment will be severe because our sins are severe. But they also point out that hundreds of verses describe future punishment in terms of "death" or "destruction" or "cutting off" or "perishing," including what is considered by many to be the most famous verse in the Bible, John 3:16, which says, "For God so loved the world that he gave his one and only Son, that whoever believes in him shall not perish but have eternal life." Those who believe receive eternal life; those who do not believe "perish."

In the same way, Jesus said, "Do not be afraid of those who kill the body but cannot kill the soul. Rather, be afraid of the One who can destroy both soul and body in hell" (Matt. 10:28). So in the future, God will "destroy" both the soul and the body of those who refuse to obey Him. That is quite different from torturing them forever. They will be destroyed—dying once and for all, never to live again—while others will enjoy eternal life—indescribably wonderful, eternal life.

These same Bible teachers understand Matthew 25:46, which we previously quoted in this chapter, to say that they (the wicked) will go away to eternal punishment—meaning a punishment that lasts forever, the forfeiting of life—but the righteous to eternal life. The contrast here is between the fate of these two groups, one which receives eternal punishment, the other which receives eternal life. The verse does not say that both will live forever, one group living in hell and the other group living in heaven. No, one group will receive an eternal punishment, namely, final destruction, the forfeiting of life. The other group will receive eternal life. That's how these teachers would understand verses like this.

It's the same with Daniel 12:2, previously mentioned. The righteous will rise from the dead to receive everlasting life; the wicked will rise to be condemned and destroyed, remembered forever for their sin. Similarly, based on this interpretation, the fire of hell does not speak of eternal torturing since it is the fire that burns forever, not the people. Fire burns things up. All that to say that there are different ways to understand the question of future punishment, based on the Bible alone.[12]

To be absolutely clear, we must not minimize the depth of human sin, the holiness of God, or the seriousness of the final judgment. Not for a second. But we must also leave room to let the Word of God speak for itself, avoiding caricatures and misconceptions. And we must not let outside traditions, be they Jewish or Christian or simply part of the culture, influence how we understand the issues of hell and future judgment.

For me, having wrestled with these issues for more than fifty years and studied the relevant verses in minute detail, what gives me comfort and assurance is knowing the mercy, kindness, and love of my heavenly Father. I know the depth of grace that pours out of the heart of the Lord Jesus. I know how extraordinarily patient and kind He has been to me throughout my life and how slow He is to bring judgment. That's why when I wonder what will happen to my own parents on that day, or to devout rabbis I have dialogued with for years, or to caring mothers living in remote villages who never heard of the Lord, I rest assured in this: my God will do what is right, and neither I nor any other person on the planet will be able to raise a word of righteous protest. He will be utterly blameless then as well as forever.

CHAPTER 10

CAN DECONSTRUCTION
BE HEALTHY?

S IT HEALTHY to question what you believe? Is it good to examine the sources of your faith? Or is this a dangerous practice, a matter of opening up a Pandora's box of doubts and questions, even to the point of giving place to the devil? It all depends on the motivation of your heart and the types of questions you are asking.

If your intent is to mock, undermine, and destroy, likely you will not find the truth. You have already made up your mind, and you can easily find confirmation for your cynicism and scorn. But if you have honest questions or serious doubts, and if your intent is to get to the truth, whatever the cost or consequence, then asking these questions can be healthy indeed. Your heart and mind can be in harmony.

That said, allow me to offer some cautions. Pride is a very dangerous thing, and often an arrogance comes with learning new things. "I know something you don't know! You are so simplistic in your faith! I'm sophisticated." In reality, we who think we know something are often the ones who are ignorant, being babes in our field of learning but thinking we are so wise. We watch a few videos online, and now we are experts. We read a few books, and now we have become scholars. Be very careful here. A little humility goes a long way. In contrast, as Paul expressed it so succinctly, knowledge puffs up but love builds up (1 Cor. 8:1).

It's also true that not everything comes through academic study. Do you marry your spouse based on research and analysis or based on love? Do you give yourself to a righteous cause based on statistics or based on solidarity and empathy? Do you become friends with someone based on scientific study or based on relationship? And where does trust come into play?

Personally, I love scholarship. I love critical study. When I was in college, I studied Hebrew, Arabic, Greek, Latin, German, and Yiddish. In graduate school, I added Ugaritic, Aramaic, Syriac, Akkadian (meaning, Babylonian and Assyrian), Phoenician, and French, plus some other, smaller dialects. I love to dig deep when I study!

I have written commentaries on Jeremiah and Job, and I'm currently working on a commentary on Isaiah. My doctoral dissertation focused on *one Hebrew word*. So yes, I find great value in serious academic study, and that includes asking critical, difficult questions. As I shared earlier in the book, over the decades my studies have increased my confidence in the veracity of God's Word.

But when the Lord asks me to trust Him, it's because He has proven Himself faithful to me over these decades. My trust is based on relationship, first and foremost. And when I fall on my face and worship Him, it is because of His beauty, holiness, and goodness rather than because of an insight I gleaned about biblical Hebrew.

You say, "But that's the whole problem. You just want me to trust everything blindly. To believe the Bible because you say I should. To hold to my faith because my church does. Worse still, you threaten me with hell if I don't believe like you do. Why should I trust what you say?"

The fact is you should *not* trust blindly, nor should you believe anything because I say so. Why should you? Please understand that I am not threatening anyone with anything.

I encourage you to study and seek. I encourage you to ask probing questions. I encourage you to pursue the truth earnestly and passionately.[1] But I encourage you to do it with a right spirit, respecting those who have studied these issues for many years, understanding that it takes time and effort to master a new field, and recognizing that not everything is a matter of academic study or religious debate. As Leonard Ravenhill (1907–1994) said, "A man with an experience of God is never at the mercy of a man with an argument."

Think back to John 9 when the man born blind was healed by Jesus on the Sabbath. According to the religious authorities, Jesus could not have been sent by God because He healed on the Sabbath, in violation of their traditions. So they called the man in for questioning a first time and then a second time: "'Give glory to God by telling the truth,' they said. 'We know this man is a sinner.' He replied, 'Whether he is a sinner or not, I don't know. One thing I do know. I was blind but now I see'" (John 9:24–25)! No amount of arguing was going to change his mind, and for good reason. He had been blind his entire life, and now he could see. The person who did this for him was certainly sent by God.

It's the same thing with us, even if we have not been healed of physical blindness. In response to whatever the Lord has done in our lives in tangible, undeniable ways, He expects us to respond with faith and trust. He wants us to grow in our relationship with Him, and we dare not scorn those sacred experiences or try to explain them away. They are loving acts of a caring God. We should love Him back in response.

Now, having asked a number of former believers to recount something that appeared to be miraculous when they were in the faith—something that seemed to have no rational explanation at the time—how did they explain that apparent miracle today? Strikingly, none of them could give me a single example of any such apparent miracle or seemingly divine intervention, making me wonder how real God had been in their lives. They couldn't give me even one solid example of apparent divine intervention in all their years in the Lord? It would be one thing to say, "Back then, it really seemed like a miracle, but here's my explanation today." Instead, they could point to nothing more than good feelings or a sense of peace they once enjoyed.

Finally, one former believer told me that he had frequently experienced what appeared to be supernatural occurrences, and he gave me one example that he described as *possibly* being a coincidence, although it seemed quite a stretch to call it a coincidence. He had no answer for it, other than to say that it happened but that he no longer believed it was an instance of divine intervention. But to see things like this happen time and time again, as he claimed was the pattern of his life? To call them coincidences would be to strain credulity.

So I asked him to perform a little spiritual exercise. "Start thinking back through the years," I said, "and write down every single example of these apparent miracles that you can think of. I know you won't be able to remember every one of them, but write down whichever ones you can remember whenever they come to mind. Then look at the cumulative evidence and ask yourself if they can so easily be explained away." I have not heard from him since.

The point I'm making is that very often in the process of losing faith and deconstructing there is also a loss of perspective and reality. It's like a husband who tells his wife after thirty years of marriage, "I want a divorce. I don't love you anymore. In fact, the more I think about it, I never really loved you."

In reality, he *did* love his wife over the years, and he *was* happily married—that is, until his affair started with a gal he met at work. The more he gave his heart to her, the less he cared for his wife. The more his heart was hardened, the more distorted his perceptions became, until he rewrote the past. He literally deceived himself. The same thing can happen to us in our walk with the Lord—as our hearts become hardened, we forget the very real, very wonderful things He did for us in the past, claiming that it was all in our head. I urge you not to let this happen to you.

Go back to your journals, if you have any. Recall the things the Lord did for you. Recount the miracles if you (or close family members or friends) experienced them. Don't let your present struggles with the faith or the intimidation of intellectual-sounding arguments rob you of the truth of the past.

GOD USES THE WEAK AND FOOLISH

When I was in college, just getting my feet wet in intellectual studies and, for the first time, starting to read more widely in the larger theological world, I came across a little book by a famous German theologian named Helmut Thielicke. In the book, *A Little Exercise for Young Theologians*, Thielicke describes the arrogance of a young seminary student who sits in judgment over a simple pastor, thinking to himself (and I paraphrase), "He doesn't know Hebrew or Greek. He can't define his epistemological base. He has no clear hermeneutical guidelines. The poor soul!" But the Lord says of this simple man, "Yes, but He knows Me far better than you do!"

As it is written in Jeremiah 9:23–24, "Thus says the LORD: 'Let not the wise man boast in his wisdom, let not the mighty man boast in his might, let not the rich man boast in his riches, but let him who boasts boast in this, that he understands and knows me, that I am the LORD who practices steadfast love, justice, and righteousness in the earth. For in these things I delight, declares the LORD'" (ESV). Or as the Lord said through Isaiah, "For thus says the One who is high and lifted up, who inhabits eternity, whose name is Holy: 'I dwell in the high and holy place, and also with him who is of a contrite and lowly spirit, to revive the spirit of the lowly, and to revive the heart of the contrite'" (Isa. 57:15, ESV).

That's why Jesus often tangled with the very learned religious leaders but was embraced by the common people. The leaders trusted in their own righteousness and leaned on their own knowledge; the common people recognized their sin and leaned on Jesus.

We too must be careful not to fall into that trap, scorning the "common people"—the simple people of faith who love the Lord and serve the hurting—because they have not learned what we have learned, trusting in our own wisdom rather than recognizing our spiritual ignorance. As Paul writes (with brilliant insight):

> For the word of the cross is folly to those who are perishing, but to us who are being saved it is the power of God. For it is written, "I will destroy the wisdom of the wise, and the discernment of the discerning I will thwart."
>
> Where is the one who is wise? Where is the scribe? Where is the debater of this age? Has not God made foolish the wisdom of the world? For since, in the wisdom of God, the world did not know God through wisdom, it pleased God through the folly of what we preach to save those who believe. For Jews demand signs and Greeks seek wisdom, but we preach Christ crucified, a stumbling block to Jews and folly to Gentiles, but to those who are called, both Jews and Greeks, Christ the power of God and the wisdom of God. For the foolishness of God is wiser than men, and the weakness of God is stronger than men.
>
> —1 Corinthians 1:18–25, esv

Do you grasp the depth of these words, words that were written by a master debater, a learned scholar, a deep theologian—indeed, one of the most profound religious thinkers the world has ever seen? He continues:

> For consider your calling, brothers: not many of you were wise according to worldly standards, not many were powerful, not many were of noble birth. But God chose what is foolish in the world to shame the wise; God chose what is weak in the world to shame the strong; God chose what is low and despised in the world,

even things that are not, to bring to nothing things that are, so that no human being might boast in the presence of God. And because of him you are in Christ Jesus, who became to us wisdom from God, righteousness and sanctification and redemption, so that, as it is written, "Let the one who boasts, boast in the Lord."

—1 CORINTHIANS 1:26–31, ESV

Above all, God is looking at our hearts—at our attitudes, at what makes us tick, at who we really are. And He is far more inclined to entrust His secrets to an illiterate street sweeper who communes with Him through the day and gives of his meager income to help the poor than He is to confide in a haughty, learned professor who glories in his learning.

God is so much wiser than we are—infinitely so—that He hides His wisdom in plain sight, hanging it on a cross to the mockery of the world. As Paul also wrote, in Jesus "are hidden all the treasures of wisdom and knowledge" (Col. 2:3).

This does not mean that we turn off our brains or that we suspend logical thinking. It certainly does not mean that we stick our heads in the sand when confronted with challenges and issues, simply repeating, "God says it, I believe it, and that settles it!" To the contrary, there is a place for intensive study, for stretching our minds, for challenging our assumptions, for digging deeply into theological mysteries, for probing all kinds of exegetical, historical, apologetic, and philosophical issues. I have spent decades doing those very things, often engaging in high-level debates with scholars of other faiths (or nonfaiths). Debating is one of my favorite activities. I'm simply raising a caution here as someone who could have easily fallen into intellectual snobbism if not for God's grace.

To say it again, a little humility goes a long way, and you do well not to throw out everything you have believed just because you hit some serious bumps in the road. Really now, are you surprised that some atheists insist there is no scientific evidence for the existence of God? Are you shocked that they actually raise some strong arguments? Were you unaware that Jewish rabbis have many powerful reasons why they do not believe in Jesus? Or that Muslim apologists have their own intellectual explanations for rejecting the authority of the Bible? Or that liberal religious scholars have an intimidating array of objections to the historicity of the Gospels?

Many Christians live in such a spiritual bubble that they are unaware of the arguments against their faith, and once they become exposed to those arguments, their faith crumbles. (I was surprised to hear a former evangelical Christian, now an atheist, tell me that he really did not get exposed to strong arguments against the Bible until he was doing his PhD studies, meaning that all through college and graduate school his faith was only reinforced and never challenged. Once it was challenged in a serious way, his faith quickly collapsed. He earned his first two degrees in Christian schools. He earned his PhD in a secular university.)

For me, meeting with learned rabbis in those first years of faith and reading books that attacked my beliefs, I had nowhere to go for answers. The pastor of my church, as much as he loved the Lord, had no background whatsoever in countering these objections, and I did not know a single believing biblical scholar. Not one. That forced me to seek God all the more earnestly and study all the more deeply, committing myself afresh to honor the Lord and follow His truth wherever the journey took me. (Believing in God was not my issue;

determining whether Jesus was the Jewish Messiah was the massive question for me.)

But for me, as I have previously stated, the more I studied, the stronger my faith became, which is why I have devoted so much of my life to answering Jewish objections to Jesus. And that's why, over the years, I have debated Jewish rabbis in the public square, perhaps more than anyone else in our generation.

Yet in the process of all this study, I learned something else. I learned that simple people of faith had much to teach me as well. That God was not impressed with my knowledge, which, in His sight, is less than a spoonful of water drawn out of the ocean. That, above all, He looked to those who were contrite in heart, recognizing their own needs, faults, and lacks, walking in humility rather than strutting in pride.

So as you ask honest questions about your faith and examine the claims of Scripture, do so with a right heart. Don't believe every objection you hear just because it sounds appealing. And by all means, don't fall into the trap of wanting to appear smart and wise to others, saying to yourself, "Hey, I'm sharp too! Watch me mock the Bible! I'm one of the smart ones too!"

MEET A BRILLIANT
NEW TESTAMENT SCHOLAR

This reminds me of the story of my good friend Craig Keener, one of the most brilliant New Testament scholars in the world. When he was a teenager, already reading Greek and Latin classics in English, he professed atheism because, he thought, that's what the smart people do. Then the Lord revealed Himself to Craig, and his life was radically changed and he began attending a local church. But he soon realized that he got a late start, not being raised in a faith environment and never reading the Bible before. So he began to pore over the Scriptures, reading forty chapters a day. This meant he would read the New Testament every week and the whole Bible every month.

He then went to college and seminary, earning his PhD in New Testament Studies and the Origins of Christianity from Duke University (which, for the record, is anything but a fundamentalist school) and becoming perhaps the foremost authority today on the ancient background to the New Testament. Just check out his commentary on Acts, running to roughly six thousand pages, and work your way through the footnotes in any one of the commentary's four volumes. It would take you a lifetime to get through all the material in detail, yet Craig himself wrote all these volumes, along with many others, including an eye-opening, award-winning, two-volume book called *Miracles: The Credibility of the New Testament Accounts*.[2] In it, he exposes the spirit of rationalism that rejects miracles, despite the evidence, also documenting numerous extraordinary miracles taking place in our day.

Are you sure you know more than Craig? Have you memorized books of the New Testament in Greek? Have you read thousands of pages of ancient literature in Greek, Latin, Hebrew, and Aramaic? Have you read Craig's *Miracles* book?[3]

The point? Craig has heard every objection to the credibility and reliability of the New Testament that you have heard. He has studied with equally brilliant men and women who were skeptics rather than believers. Yet, having reviewed all the evidence, he is absolutely convinced of the truthfulness of God's Word. Perhaps you need to do some further study?

I'm quite aware that learned skeptics and learned believers

exist. But often, when we are confronted with challenges to our faith from professors, scientists, or people who seem to be in the know, we feel intimidated. "Who am I to differ with them?" we think. But that sword cuts both ways. Who are you to argue with Craig Keener (and many other brilliant biblical scholars, theologians, Christian philosophers, scientists, and researchers)? It would take some of us forty or fifty years to catch up to them—if we could even do it then. So to say it again, a little humility goes a long way, and if you want to reexamine what you believe and why, do it the right way.

The reality is that we know far less than we think we know, and when we mock the book that has brought positive change to the world, far more than any other book ever written, we expose our own ignorance.[4] Many fine people far more knowledgable than you or me, people whose lives put us to shame in terms of character, sacrifice, and service, people whose very presence would humble us, people who are smarter than us in their sleep—these very people have read this same Bible and encountered the same objections and dealt with the same challenges in life. Yet they have remained strong in their faith and their love for the Lord, not by shutting off their minds, but by opening their hearts and expanding their minds.

If that's what deconstruction does for you, stripping away the false from the true and grounding you more deeply in the Lord, then it is a good and healthy process. But if it means becoming arrogant toward other believers, judgmental in your attitude, a cynic and a skeptic and a mocker, then no, it has done infinitely more harm than good.

If you say, "But that's where the evidence leads," I beg to differ—and I say that with all respect and with more than fifty years of asking the tough questions, welcoming the difficult objections, and experiencing the ups and downs of life. God remains our rock and refuge, and His Word remains as reliable and sure as ever. Perhaps you have not yet arrived at your final destination? Perhaps you need to continue on your journey in pursuit of the truth?

ONE LAST WORD OF CAUTION

John Cooper, lead singer and front man of the Christian rock band Skillet, has become a very good friend in the last couple of years. He has taken a very strong stand against the deconstruction movement, specifically, against former believers who have become mockers (as opposed to those who are really struggling with their faith and wrestling with difficult issues).[5] In 2022, he shared with me that he was interacting with a Christian woman who told him that she was deconstructing, although, she made clear, she still considered herself a Christian.

As they talked, he showed her that she had gone further down the path of unbelief than she realized, to the point of denying some of the fundamentals of the faith. This was a real eye-opener for her. Not only so, but when John probed her on various social issues, she explained that her views had changed on these too. This, in turn, led to a fascinating insight.

Why, John asked her, did her new views, without exception, correspond to the current talking points of the Left? Why was it that, in each and every case, her reading of the Bible now agreed with the perspectives of those who did not believe? Why, in her pursuit of spiritual truth, had she come into deep harmony with the world, meaning, with the spirit of the age? Her eyes were now opened wide.

You see, it's easy to get swept away with the tide of the hour, with the prevailing wind of the day. It's easy to be seduced into appearing to be woke, demonstrating to the watching world that we are so enlightened and in touch, not like those Bible-thumping, small-minded, bigoted believers. We are not like them! As a result, in our rejection of our previous beliefs, some of which might be outdated and outmoded, we exchange the religion of fundamentalism for the religion of progressivism, discarding the older traditions for the newer traditions.

So if you find yourself accepted by the woke and progressive crowd, let alone celebrated by them, beware. In the days ahead, if you truly pursue what is right and good and upright and liberating and full of truth, you will have to deconstruct again. You might even find yourself sitting with your old pastor again (or your godly mother or father), the one whose beliefs you scorned and openly mocked—"How naïve and simplistic he is!"—asking him or her from your heart, "Could you tell me more about Jesus? I see that, above all, I really need Him."

CHAPTER 11

WHERE DO WE GO
FROM HERE?

WHY HAVE YOU read this book? Only you can answer that question. Why did I write this book? I can answer that! I wrote it to help clarify why so many Christians are leaving the faith, as stated in the title. And I wrote it to help strengthen those who are struggling with their faith (or who have left the faith entirely). Has this book helped you? Has it strengthened your faith? Has it opened your eyes? Has it given you cause for hope? Has it brought you back to your faith? Only you can answer those questions.

For my part, I have sought to be totally honest and candid, at times brutally so. I have not minimized the sins of the church or the challenges of walking with the Lord in this world. At the same time, I have presented honest and candid responses to each and every problem and challenge, responses that I believe will stand the test of time. With all my heart, soul, and mind, I am absolutely convinced that God and His

Word are trustworthy. And while I hope that, either now or in the future, that will be your conviction as well, that is not up to me. I can only ask you to be honest with yourself as you continue on your journey. The fact that you have taken the time to read this book, especially if you have deconstructed, is a great step in the right direction.

I also recognize that spirituality is a complex thing, just as we humans are complex beings. We are physical and intellectual. We are social and emotional. We are influenced by our environment and genetics. We can be rational and irrational.

When it comes to our spirituality, one powerful experience can change us for life, bringing us into a relationship with God that we never question again for the rest of our days. Or one bad experience can damage us for life, making us question whether God really exists. Some of us seem to be 90 percent heart and 10 percent mind when it comes to our relationship with the Lord, while others seem to be the reverse. Some of us seem to have childlike faith, finding it natural and easy to trust God, while others try so hard to believe and yet can never seem to muster any real faith. Where do you fit on this spectrum?

Recently, a pastor told me about a couple in his congregation with a blended family, with both the husband and wife suffering divorces in their past before they married each other, each of them bringing children from their previous marriages. Then, once married, within a short time, both of them lost one of their children, first the husband, then the wife. Talk about overwhelming tragedies. As the saying goes, parents are not meant to bury their children.

The wife was so devastated that she lost her faith entirely. So the pastor asked her to read my book *Has God Failed You?*

Finding Faith When You're Not Even Sure God Is Real. (For obvious reasons, I've referenced that book a few times already in the previous pages.) As a result of reading the book, her faith was restored and she is now strong again in the Lord.

In sharp contrast, shortly before the pastor shared this story with me, a friend of mine sent the same book to his son, an atheist who openly mocks religion. My friend is a few years older than me and the CEO of a large Christian ministry. His son is in his forties, quite firm in his unbelief. But for some reason he was willing to read my book. What was his response? He sent snide texts to his dad, judging me to be insincere and manipulative. Same book, very different results!

Again, for my part, I can assure you that every word I write is sincere and that the last thing I want to do is manipulate anyone spiritually, emotionally, or intellectually. That's why when I'm invited to address a controversial topic on a college campus, I request that those inviting me find someone who is willing to debate the issue with me. Rather than just giving a lecture, I want the audience to hear the opposing side. That way, having heard both sides for themselves, audience members can come to a more solid conclusion.

It's the same thing with this book. I'm encouraging you to do further study. But I'm urging you to do so with a humble, sincere heart and a genuinely open mind. I'm also encouraging you to remember the things the Lord has done in your life—if you are or were a believer—and not to rewrite the past based on your current state of mind. Just because He may seem distant in the present doesn't mean He didn't work miracles in your life in the past.

Above all, do not let your peers' influence or others' perceptions determine your life decisions. One day, whether you believe it or not, you will stand before God and give account to Him—not to your friends on social media, not to your pastor or parents, and certainly not to me. Whatever decisions you make and whatever conclusions you reach, be sure you are ready to live for them and die with them.

Where, then, do we go from here? Having prayed over the contents of this book, I'm going to share a few final thoughts. My goal? To leave you with a greater sense of confidence in the truth of the gospel. Shall we continue?

ONE LESS GOD?

Atheists like Stephen Roberts say to monotheists (people who believe there is only one God), "I contend that we are both atheists, I just believe in one fewer god than you do. When you understand why you dismiss all the other possible gods, you will understand why I dismiss yours."[1] Or, as others have expressed it, "You're an atheist with respect to Zeus, Poseidon, Jupiter, etc. which means you're an atheist like me! It's just that I believe in one less god than you."[2]

But that's the thing. This "one less god" is the only true God. The rest were frauds and shams, here today and gone tomorrow. But the only God—the Creator and sustainer of the universe—is from everlasting to everlasting. We rightly reject the counterfeits. We wrongly reject the real and true.

Interestingly, God already addressed this in the Bible, saying that the gods of the nations—Marduk, Baal, Asherah, Zeus, Poseidon, and Jupiter—were not really gods at all and that He alone was God. He said in His Word that He alone would endure through the ages and the other "gods" would be no more. And that's exactly what has happened. Consequently, in their zeal to reject the false gods, the ones who are not gods at all, these atheists have rejected the true God, the one and only God. So it's not a matter of "one less god." It's a matter of an infinite number of false gods, none of whom should be worshipped or feared, in absolute contrast with the eternal, true, and only God, who alone is worthy of worship and reverence.

The Bible actually acknowledges the existence of these "gods," but it explains that they are not eternal or all-powerful or all-wise or all-knowing. Instead, it identifies them as demons—deceiving spirits claiming to be divine, known to the world as Zeus or Baal or Krishna. People have bowed down to them and revered them as deities. People have offered sacrifices to them and lived in fear of their power. But the Bible told us millennia ago that *they were not gods at all* and, more importantly, *that there is only one true God.*

The other so-called gods were simply deceiving spirits masquerading as gods, similar to the Wizard of Oz hiding behind his scary, false image. The Bible exposed them as frauds, just as Toto exposed the Wizard. And the Bible made clear that long after these other gods were forgotten and their images buried in the dust, the God of the Bible would still be worshipped. That's because only He is God.

And so the "one less" argument of the atheists actually works against them, since all the other "gods," who have rightly faded into oblivion, were never gods at all. The God of the Bible, worshipped by more people today than at any other point in world history, is the only true God. He told us that the other so-called gods were—and are—a sham. The sham has been exposed!

Consider verses like these, spoken before and after the exodus from Egypt (emphasis added):

- "On that same night I will pass through Egypt and strike down every firstborn of both people and animals, and *I will bring judgment on all the gods of Egypt. I am the* LORD" (Exod. 12:12).

- "*Who among the gods is like you,* LORD? Who is like you—majestic in holiness, awesome in glory, working wonders" (Exod. 15:11)?

- "*Now I know that the* LORD *is greater than all other gods,* for he did this to those who had treated Israel arrogantly" (Exod. 18:11).

That's why, about forty years later, Moses said, "For the LORD your God is *God of gods and Lord of lords,* the great God, mighty and awesome, who shows no partiality and accepts no bribes" (Deut. 10:17, emphasis added). That's why the psalmist proclaimed, "For you, LORD, are the *Most High* over all the earth; *you are exalted far above all gods*" (Ps. 97:9, emphasis added; note that the very title "Most High" means that the Lord is higher than every other "god"). That's why King Hezekiah stated, "*They have thrown their gods into the fire and destroyed them, for they were not gods but only wood and stone, fashioned by human hands*" (Isa. 37:19, emphasis added).

And that's why Paul explained:

We know that "An idol is nothing at all in the world" and that "There is no God but one." For even if there are so-called gods, whether in heaven or on earth (as indeed there are many "gods" and many "lords"), yet for us there is but one God, the Father, from whom all things came and for whom we live; and there is but one Lord, Jesus Christ, through whom all things came and through whom we live.

—1 Corinthians 8:4–6

He also stated that "the sacrifices of pagans are offered to demons, not to God, and I do not want you to be participants with demons" (1 Cor. 10:20).

So in the Bible itself God acknowledged the existence of these other "gods" who were worshipped by the peoples of the earth. But He also said to them, "You are not gods at all. You cannot predict the future. You cannot give life or take life away. You are no more powerful than the idols made to represent you. I alone am God!"

With good reason, then, we have discarded all these other so-called gods, choosing to worship and acknowledge the one and only God, the Lord Himself. And so the atheists who use the "one less god" argument have it totally backward. While rightly rejecting the counterfeits, they have thrown out the genuine. While recognizing the false gods as nothing, they have failed to acknowledge the one true God as everything. He alone is the Creator, and He alone has immortality. Everything else has been created by Him, and everything else ceases to exist the moment He withdraws His sustaining hand.

NOT JUST THE GOD OF THE BIBLE BUT THE BIBLE ITSELF

But it's not just the God of the Bible who has endured. The Bible itself has stood the test of time. In fact, it was reported in 2022 that "on average there are 100 million Bibles printed each year," and, "It's projected that there are more than

6 billion Bibles currently in print—140% more than the estimated 2.5 billion copies in print as of 1975."[3] Why are so many people still reading the Bible? Why does it continue to be the world's best-selling book year after year?

I'm quite aware that popularity doesn't equal truth and that, while not as popular as the Bible, the Quran is studied and read by hundreds of millions of Muslims. But if you would listen to some skeptics and mockers, atheists and nonbelievers, you would think that the Bible is its own worst enemy. In the words of Hemant Mehta, editor of the *Friendly Atheist* blog, "[Richard] Dawkins and [Dan] Barker have both written books encouraging readers to become atheists. Who knew all they had to do was direct everyone to the Bible?"[4]

Why is it, then, that billions of people, including some of the most brilliant, learned people on the planet, along with the simple and the lowly, continue to feast on the riches of this book? Why do so many find inspiration, purpose, direction, correction, edification, guidance, hope, and more in the pages of the Scriptures? If the Bible is so bad, so outdated, so cruel, so bigoted, so filled with error, so obviously and fatally flawed, why does it gain more readers every year?

What may be the most popular Bible app is YouVersion, available for free on most major platforms. Its website reported this in 2022:

> As some churches temporarily paused physical services to stop the spread of COVID-19, many people used digital tools to connect with God, including the Bible App. With 43.6 billion Bible chapters read, 7.5 billion audio chapters played, and 1.4 billion Bible Plan days completed, the YouVersion Bible App saw its highest levels of global Bible engagement in app history.[5]

In the same post, the site also reported that it had "experienced record-breaking growth" for a kids' Bible app, citing, "In 2020 alone, the app was installed on more than 22 million unique devices, totaling more than 60 million devices worldwide."

Again, popularity doesn't equal truth. But when countless millions of people—many of them former atheists and agnostics—find spiritual riches in the pages of this Book, and when they testify to the tremendous, positive changes they have experienced by following the counsel of this Book, it is both ignorant and arrogant to write all of them off as deceived and delusional.

If you yourself have rejected the Bible, are you also ready to say that all those who revere the Scriptures are superstitious? Or uninformed? Or simpleminded? Or blind? Or bound by fear and tradition? Or biased? Or brainwashed? All of them? Are you sure?

Again, I'm quite aware that some brilliant historians and textual scholars reject the Bible on factual grounds, not spiritual grounds. They find it historically inaccurate and filled with textual errors. But there are equally brilliant historians and textual scholars who embrace the Bible *because of* its factual accuracy, finding it confirmed by archeology, in harmony with ancient historical records, and preserved with amazing care. In the same way, there are brilliant philosophers who take strong moral exception to the Bible. But there are equally brilliant philosophers who embrace the Bible because of its exceptional morality. To be quite blunt, you deceive yourself if you think, "Only uneducated and unthinking people believe the Bible today." Not so!

And why do you think the Bible is also the world's most

banned book?[6] Why do you think Diocletian, the Roman emperor, *burned* copies of the Bible? It is not for the reasons given by the atheists, who reject it as bigoted and outdated. Rather it has been banned and burned because it is a threat to oppressive governments, be they totalitarian Communist governments or fundamentalist Islamic regimes. It is because the Bible is a book of liberation and emancipation, a book that recognizes the dignity of each human being, with all of us created in God's image, a book that points to an authority higher than that of presidents and prime ministers and dictators and emperors and religious tyrants. (That includes "Christian" religious tyrants too!) No wonder so many consider it to be a dangerous book. Its ideas are too liberating!

In short, the fact that the Bible remains so incredibly popular today, that it continues to change lives in so many positive ways (the stories we hear regularly are deeply moving and often inspirational), and that some of us have been studying its contents for decades and continue to be amazed at its hidden treasures, should at least give some pause for thought. Perhaps there's something that is being missed? Perhaps, before dismissing and dissing the Bible, you should take a second (or third or fourth) look?

I have sometimes heard a comedian telling jokes and said to myself, "That guy is not funny at all. I can't believe he draws such big crowds. And why is everyone laughing?" After a while, I say to myself, "Maybe I'm just not getting his jokes!"

Could it be, then, that when it comes to the Bible, some of us are misunderstanding what it's really about? Could it be that it contains treasures waiting to be unearthed but we have not taken the time to dig? Or do you think it's just a coincidence that more than twenty-five hundred years ago God said that His words would always endure? As it is written in Isaiah: "A voice says, 'Cry out.' And I said, 'What shall I cry?' 'All people are like grass, and all their faithfulness is like the flowers of the field. The grass withers and the flowers fall, because the breath of the LORD blows on them. Surely the people are grass. The grass withers and the flowers fall, but the word of our God endures forever'" (40:6–8).

Isn't it interesting that *these* words are being studied and memorized today rather than the words of other ancient Near Eastern books? And isn't it ironic that we're reading the words of this same God who called out all the other so-called gods as frauds and shams rather than reading the words of those other "gods"?

And what do we make of this statement made by Jesus, especially when we remember that He was a humble carpenter from an obscure little town who died a shameful criminal's death? "Heaven and earth will pass away, but my words will never pass away" (Matt. 24:35). Really now, you would have to be pretty deluded or arrogant to make such a claim—unless you were really the Lord! The fact is, when a person told you twenty centuries ago that their words would never pass away, and then, twenty centuries later, that person's words are the most quoted words on the planet, this should give us pause for thought. Who *was* this man Jesus? Could it be He *was* more than a man?

Speaking of Jesus, why do you think *The Jesus Film*, which is a simple retelling of the gospel story, is reportedly the most translated film in world history? As one site notes, "The movie's cumulative viewing and listening audience (multiple viewings plus Internet viewings) tops 6.2 billion. Almost 200 million people have indicated they came to faith in Christ after viewing the film. It has been seen in 238 countries in 848 languages, making it the world's most translated film."[7] What makes Jesus so attractive to so many people in so many cultures over so many centuries? Are you sure you want to walk away from *Him*?

To this moment, Christians around the world are suffering imprisonment, torture, deprivation, and death because of their loyalty to this same Jesus. But He has been so true to them, so real to them, so beautiful to them, that they would rather die than deny Him. Do you know this same Jesus for yourself? Or in the past, when you used to be a believer, are you sure you really knew Him? If not, getting to know Him up close and personal should be the paramount goal of your life.

FLEEING *FROM* GOD *TO* GOD

In John 6, Jesus gave a very difficult teaching, sharing some truths that could easily be misunderstood but that also exposed the wrong motivation of many of His followers. As a result, John wrote, "Many of his disciples turned back and no longer followed him." It was a mass exodus. So Jesus asked His twelve core disciples, "You do not want to leave too, do you?" Peter replied, "Lord, to whom shall we go? You have the words of eternal life. We have come to believe and to know that you are the Holy One of God" (John 6:66–69).

Peter was saying in essence, "We don't understand everything You said either. But we know who You are, and we have nowhere else to go. Only You have the words of eternal life."

But this is not the talk of cultlike, close-minded devotion. These are not the sentiments of the brainwashed. Instead, this is how people talk when they have really encountered Jesus. They have seen Him in action, healing the sick, raising the dead, liberating the oppressed, exposing religious hypocrisy, bringing people near to God, forgiving their sins, changing their lives, doing what no one else in world history ever did. These same disciples also saw Jesus die on the cross, then rise from the dead, then ascend into heaven, and then send His Spirit so they could do the same things He did. Who could possibly talk them out of that?

That's why almost all of these same men—the initial, faithful eleven disciples—subsequently died for their faith rather than deny their Lord. Faced with the choice of renouncing the King who laid down His life for them or being tortured and put to death themselves, they joyfully embraced torture and death. Tradition even teaches that this same Peter, the one who said, "Lord, to whom shall we go? You have the words of eternal life" (John 6:68), was crucified upside down, not feeling worthy to be crucified in the same way His Master was.

Peter's words speak to us to this very day: To whom else can we go? Who else has the words of eternal life? Who else can replace Jesus? Perhaps the church has failed you. Perhaps your closest Christian friends have let you down. Perhaps your pastor has sinned against you. But Jesus has not failed you or let you down or sinned against you. Run back to Him, and rebuild your life from there. Everything else will fall back into place as you do.

This is something Job learned as well. He was the godliest man on the planet, singled out by the Lord for his piety. And he was abundantly blessed by God with tremendous wealth, a great, big family, and a wonderful reputation. But during an intense spiritual test, everything was taken from him: his wealth, his reputation, his health, and worst of all, his ten children—all of them! And this happened in a very short time.

How did he respond? Initially, he simply praised and worshipped God, saying that the Lord gave and the Lord took away. His faith remained strong. But as the days went on and his well-meaning friends began to share their theology with him, Job's tune began to change. (If you really want to dig deeply into this amazing book, I've written a full-length commentary on it. If you want a one-chapter overview of Job, you'll find that in *Has God Failed You?*)[8]

Job's friends first suggested that he was, in fact, a righteous man but that he had some serious flaws, because of which God was teaching him a lesson by putting him through this time of chastisement and correction. But Job knew this was not the case. This was not a loving correction from the hands of his heavenly Father. This was a brutal assault. God needed to be challenged.

But as Job began to air his doubts and bring his open challenges to the Lord, the friends came to a new conclusion: Job, you are obviously a wicked sinner, and God is giving you what you deserve! Your children were no different. They obviously died for their sins!

These charges then triggered an even fiercer response from Job, who knew this was not the case. Did wicked sinners deserve punishments like this? Absolutely. But Job knew he was anything but a wicked sinner. He had feared God and turned from evil, living an exemplary life of faith and obedience. If there was something wrong, he concluded, it was on God's side, not his.

At the same time, there was only one place he could go, and that was to God. As some have expressed it, Job fled *from* God *to* God. He ran from the God he thought was oppressing him to the God he knew could deliver him. He appealed to

God for justice while accusing God of being unjust. (Yes, all this is written in the pages of the Bible. The biblical authors pulled no punches, and the Lord wanted us to know that He gets it. He fully understands what we go through and how we sometimes feel.)

In the end, the Lord revealed Himself to Job, exposing Job's total ignorance of how He ran the universe. God basically said, "Who are you, Job, to talk to Me about justice? You don't have the slightest clue." As a result, Job humbled himself and recanted. But then something surprising happened. The Lord commended Job for *speaking rightly about God* while rebuking the friends for *speaking wrongly about God*. Talk about turning the tables!

The friends, who seemed to be so orthodox in their beliefs, stating that God judged the wicked but blessed the righteous, were rebuked by the Lord. They were all head and no heart, holding to their rigid theology while wrongly judging a righteous man in his agony. As for Job, despite overstepping his bounds and falsely accusing the Lord of being evil, he also recognized that this same Lord would do right and that ultimately there would be justice in His universe. This Lord would one day deliver him! And He did, blessing Job far more for the rest of his life than he was blessed in the first part of his life. Even more importantly, Job came to know the Lord much more intimately and personally.

Perhaps this is where you find yourself today. You have hit bottom and feel as if you cannot believe anymore. But you don't feel right just walking away. Where, then, do you go? You want to pray, but you're not even sure there is a God. What do you do? Pray anyway. Run to the God you want to be there and you hope will be there. If He's not real, you have lost nothing by trying. If He is real—and He is!—you lose everything by leaving Him behind. He, for His part, fully understands your struggles—remember that, in Jesus, He lived in this world and was tempted and suffered pain and rejection—and He will not turn you away.

NOT TRIED AND NOT FOUND WANTING

This leads me to a wise observation from a wise man named G. K. Chesterton (1874–1936), perhaps the most quoted Christian of the last century. It was Chesterton who wrote, "The Christian ideal has not been tried and found wanting. It has been found difficult; and left untried."[9] Precisely so!

Truth be told, many have left the faith without really "trying" the faith—meaning, giving themselves fully and totally to God, throwing themselves in heart and soul, doing what Jesus actually calls us to do, getting us out of our comfort zones and taking the plunge.

Truth be told, following Jesus is not easy. It is deeply challenging. In many ways it is downright impossible. But that is part of the gospel. We come to the end of ourselves. We recognize that we cannot keep God's standards. We learn that we are more sinful, more selfish, more fleshly, more carnal than we understood. We realize that we need a Savior—and then He comes and saves us!

Have you yourself come to that breaking point? Have you arrived at the place of desperation, that place where you won't let go of God until He blesses you, precisely because you cannot let go?

It is an uncomfortable place to be—a deeply uncomfortable place. But it is also a place of liberation and freedom. When we come to the end of ourselves, we come to the beginning of His grace. As Paul wrote, God's power is made perfect through our weakness, because of which he was able to say, "When I am weak, then I am strong." (See 2 Corinthians 12:1–10.) It took me many years to learn the meaning of those words, but it has been a wonderful lesson well worth learning.

John G. Lake (1870–1935), once a very successful businessman, left America to serve as a missionary in South Africa and returned to America some years after his wife (and the mother of their seven children) reportedly died as a result of malnutrition. He was deeply familiar with pain and suffering, not only watching his own wife die, but also watching eight of his fifteen siblings die in the first decades of his life. But Lake was a man who came to know God intimately and reportedly saw thousands of people miraculously healed.

It was Lake who also said this: "No matter what your soul may be coveting, if it becomes the supreme cry of your life, not the secondary matter, or the third or fourth, the fifth or tenth, but the supreme desire of your soul, the paramount issue—all the powers and energies of your spirit, soul and body are reaching out and crying out to God for the answer—it is going to come!"[10]

Let that cry rise from your heart, the cry that says: "God, if You are there, I must know You for myself! If this gospel message is true, I must experience its full power! Nothing is more important than knowing the truth about You and the Bible. I can no longer live on the sidelines, stuck in the mud of spiritual passivity. I cannot endure any more double-mindedness, a believer one day and a cynic the next. It's either yes or no, in or out, truth or falsehood, the most amazing story of all time or just a fairy tale. God, I'm crying out to You, and I will not stop crying out and seeking and pursuing until I know that I know that I know."

My friend, if you will do this, as I have done, you will never be disappointed, not in this world and not in the next. As God Himself promised the children of Israel, "And you will seek Me and find *Me*, when you search for Me with all your heart" (Jer. 29:13, NKJV).

And no matter how well you may know the Lord and no matter how deeply you have experienced His goodness and grace, there is more to be known and more to be had. As Paul wrote: "Oh, the depth of the riches of the wisdom and knowledge of God! How unsearchable his judgments, and his paths beyond tracing out! 'Who has known the mind of the Lord? Or who has been his counselor?' 'Who has ever given to God, that God should repay them?' For from him and through him and for him are all things. To him be the glory forever! Amen" (Rom. 11:33–36).[11]

Or to share one last quote from the closing verses of the Bible, "And the Spirit and the bride say, 'Come!' And let the one who hears say: 'Come!' And let the one who is thirsty come; let the one who wants it take the water of life free of charge" (Rev. 22:17, NET). The door is still open to you!

RESOURCES TO BUILD YOUR FAITH

I HAVE PUT TOGETHER an extensive list of recommended websites, articles, and books that you can access at https://askdrbrown.org/recommendedresources. Here I have listed just a few of the most helpful websites for seekers, doubters, those questioning their faith, and those wrestling with unwanted sexual attractions and desires.

- Talk About Doubts, talkaboutdoubts.com (provides one-on-one dialogue with experts)

- CrossExamined.org (with Frank Turek)

- Cold-Case Christianity With J. Warner and Jimmy Wallace, coldcasechristianity.com

- Reasonable Faith With William Lane Craig, www.reasonablefaith.org.

- Stand to Reason: Clear-Thinking Christianity, www.str.org/home (founded by Greg Koukl)

- Apologetics 315, apologetics315.com (gathers thousands of resources)

- Sean McDowell: Bringing Truth to a New Generation, seanmcdowell.org

- Discovery Institute, www.discovery.org (intelligent design think tank)

- Restored Hope Network, www.restoredhopenetwork.org (resources related to LGBTQ+ issues)

- YouVersion, www.bible.com (a great app to get you reading the Bible)

NOTES

CHAPTER 1

1. Joshua Bote, "He Wrote the Christian Case Against Dating. Now He's Splitting From His Wife and Faith," *USA Today*, July 29, 2019, https://www.usatoday.com/story/news/nation/2019/07/29/joshua-harris-i-kissed-dating-goodbye-i-am-not-christian/1857934001/.

2. Tod Perry, "Christian 'Purity' Leader Joshua Harris Distances Himself From His Faith and Apologizes to LGBTQ Community," August 7, 2019, Upworthy, https://www.upworthy.com/joshua-harris-lgbtq-apology.

3. Michael Brown, "Reaching Out to a Hillsong Leader Who Is Renouncing His Faith," The Stream, August 12, 2019, https://stream.org/reaching-hillsong-leader-renouncing-faith/.

4. Leah MarieAnn Klett, "Hillsong Worship Leader Clarifies He Hasn't Renounced Faith, But It's on 'Incredibly Shaky Ground,'" *The Christian Post*, August 13, 2019, https://www.christianpost.com/news/hillsong-worship-leader-clarifies-he-hasnt-renounced-faith-but-its-on-incredibly-shaky-ground.html?uid=f5d32e0e40&utm_source=The+Christian+Post+List&utm_campaign=07fa2459ca-EMAIL_CAMPAIGN_2019_08_13_04_07&utm_medium=email&utm_term=0_dce2601630-07fa2459ca-4137697.

5. "'It Was Amazing Being One of You, but I'm Not Any More,' Says Hillsong's Marty Sampson," Christian Today, August 23, 2019, https://www.christiantoday.com/article/it-was-amazing-being-one-of-you-but-im-not-any-more-says-marty-sampson/133089.htm.

6. Leah MarieAnn Klett, "Hillsong Writer: 'I'm Genuinely Losing My Faith,'" *The Christian Post*, August 12, 2019, https://www.christianpost.com/news/

hillsong-writer-reveals-hes-no-longer-a-christian-im-
genuinely-losing-my-faith.html.

7. Brown, "Reaching Out."

8. Gregory A. Smith, "About Three-in-Ten U.S. Adults
   Are Now Religiously Unaffiliated," Pew Research
   Center, December 14, 2021, https://www.pewresearch.
   org/religion/2021/12/14/about-three-in-ten-u-s-adults-
   are-now-religiously-unaffiliated/#:~:text=Christians%20
   now%20outnumber%20religious%20
   %E2%80%9Cnones,Christianity%20are%20
   concentrated%20among%20Protestants.

9. Lisa Respers France, "Jonathan Steingard, Christian
   Singer, Reveals He No Longer Believes in God," CNN,
   May 27, 2020, https://www.cnn.com/2020/05/27/
   entertainment/jonathan-steingard-atheist/index.html.

10. France, "Jonathan Steingard, Christian Singer."

11. ASKDrBrown, "That's Debatable Episode 1: Jon
    Steingard," YouTube, October 20, 2022, https://youtu.be/
    ZKX6shd6ocA.

12. Jesse T. Jackson, "Former Desiring God Writer Paul
    Maxwell Renounces His Christian Faith," Church Leaders,
    April 12, 2021, https://churchleaders.com/news/394316-
    former-desiring-god-writer-paul-maxwell-renounces-his-
    christian-faith.html.

13. Michael Brown, "Responding to Brady 'Phanatik'
    Goodwin, the Latest Christian Leader to Renounce His
    Faith," The Stream, January 23, 2022, https://stream.
    org/responding-to-brady-phanatik-goodwin-the-latest-
    christian-leader-to-renounce-his-faith/.

14. Brady Phanatik Goodwin, "Unbecoming A Believer:
    Are the rumors true?," Facebook, January 17, 2022,
    https://www.facebook.com/brady.p.goodwin.1/
    posts/3769289496630504.

15. Josh Shepherd, "Pioneering Christian Hip-Hop Artist
    Phanatik Renounces His Faith," The Roys Report, January
    19, 2022, https://julieroys.com/phanatik-christian-hip-hop-
    artist-renounces-faith/.

16. Smith, "About Three-in-Ten."

17. Smith, "About Three-in-Ten."
18. "Why America's 'Nones' Don't Identify With a Religion" Pew Research Center, August 18, 2018, https://www. pewresearch.org/fact-tank/2018/08/08/why-americas-nones-dont-identify-with-a-religion/.
19. Brown, "Responding to Brady."
20. Brown, "Responding to Brady."
21. Brown, "Responding to Brady."
22. Brown, "Responding to Brady."
23. Brown, "Responding to Brady."

CHAPTER 2

1. Wikipedia, s.v. "Exvangelical," accessed October 25, 2022, https://en.wikipedia.org/wiki/Exvangelical.
2. See especially Matthew 24:3–12; 2 Thessalonians 2:3.
3. Josh McDowell Author Page, Amazon, accessed October 25, 2022, https://www.amazon.com/Josh-McDowell/e/B000APEQR8%3Fref=dbs_a_mng_rwt_scns_share.
4. Steven Poole, "The Four Horsemen Review—Whatever Happened to 'New Atheism'?" *The Guardian*, January 31, 2019, https://www.theguardian.com/books/2019/jan/31/four-horsemen-review-what-happened-to-new-atheism-dawkins-hitchens.
5. For a useful summary, see Wikipedia, s.v. *"Breaking the Spell* (Dennett book)," accessed October 25, 2022, https://en.wikipedia.org/wiki/Breaking_the_Spell_(Dennett_book).
6. "The God Delusion (Richard Dawkins)," Bible Answers, accessed October 25, 2022, http://www.bibleanswers.ie/evidences/275-the-god-delusion.
7. Richard Dawkins (@RichardDawkins), "Just learned that sales of The God Delusion have topped 3 million," Twitter, September 3, 2014, https://twitter.com/richarddawkins/status/507092728409522176.
8. Wikipedia, s.v. "God Is Not Great," accessed October 25, 2022, https://en.wikipedia.org/wiki/God_Is_Not_Great#Sales_history.

9. Sam Harris, *The End of Faith* (New York, NY: W. W. Norton & Company, 2005), 72.

10. Jennifer Schuessler, "Philosophy That Stirs the Waters," *New York Times*, April 30, 2013, https://www.nytimes. com/2013/04/30/books/daniel-dennett-author-of-intuition-pumps-and-other-tools-for-thinking.html.

11. Cited in Alister E. McGrath, *Christianity: An Introduction, Second Edition* (Malden, MA: Blackwell Publishing, 2006), 102.

12. Christopher Hitchens, "The Lord and the Intellectuals," *Harper's Magazine*, July 1982, https://harpers.org/ archive/1982/07/the-lord-and-the-intellectuals/.

13. Richard Dawkins, *The God Delusion* (New York: Mariner Books, 2008), 51.

14. Dan Barker, *God: The Most Unpleasant Character in All Fiction* (New York: Union Square & Co., 2016).

15. "Quotable Quote (Christopher Hitchens)," Goodreads, accessed October 25, 2022, https://www.goodreads.com/ quotes/325436-we-keep-on-being-told-that-religion-whatever-its-imperfections.

16. "Josh McDowell and the Quest for Da Vinci," CBN.com, accessed October 6, 2022, https://www1.cbn.com/700club/ josh-mcdowell-and-quest-da-vinci.

17. *The God Who Wasn't There*, IMDB, accessed October 25, 2022, https://www.imdb.com/title/tt0455507/.

18. "What Is the Blasphemy Challenge?" Got Questions, accessed October 25, 2022, https://www.gotquestions.org/ blasphemy-challenge.html.

19. Michael L. Brown, *Saving a Sick America: A Prescription for Moral and Cultural Transformation* (Nashville: Thomas Nelson, 2017), 44.

20. Bart D. Ehrman, *Misquoting Jesus: The Story Behind Who Changed the Bible and Why* (New York: HarperOne, 2005).

21. F. F. Bruce, *The New Testament Documents: Are They Reliable?* (Downers Grove, IL: InterVarsity, 1960), 11.

22. James Prothro, "Myths About Classical Literature: Responsibly Comparing the New Testament to Ancient

Works," in Elijah Hixson, Peter J. Gurry. eds., *Myths and Mistakes in New Testament Textual Criticism* (Downers Grove, IL: InterVarsity Press, 2019), 81 and 86, citing Giorgio Pasquali, *Storia della tradizione e critica del testo*, 2nd ed. (Florence: Le Monnier, 1952), 8.

23. Daniel Wallace, lecture, December 6, 2013, at Discover the Evidence, cited in Josh McDowell and Sean McDowell, PhD, *Evidence That Demands a Verdict*, updated and expanded ed. (Nashville, TN: Thomas Nelson, 2017), 53.

24. Tamler Sommers, "Can an Atheist Believe in Free Will?," *Psychology Today*, January 22, 2009, https://www.psychologytoday.com/us/blog/experiments-in-philosophy/200901/can-atheist-believe-in-free-will.

25. J. D. Greear, "If There Is No God, There Is No Free Will," J. D. Greear Ministries, September 26, 2017, https://jdgreear.com/blog/no-god-no-free-will.

26. Denyse O'Leary, "Using Clever Analogies, Philosopher Daniel Dennett Argues That Consciousness Is All Smoke and Mirrors," *Mind Matters*, January 21, 2019, https://mindmatters.ai/2019/01/has-science-shown-that-consciousness-is-only-an-illusion/.

27. Anna Buckley, "Is Consciousness Just an Illusion?," BBC News, April 4, 2017, https://www.bbc.com/news/science-environment-39482345.

28. "Quotable Quote (Steven Pinker)," Goodreads, accessed October 25, 2022, https://www.goodreads.com/quotes/6976574-computation-has-finally-demystified-mentalistic-terms-beliefs-are-inscriptions-in.

29. Some of the preceding paragraphs were adapted from Michael L. Brown, *Has God Failed You? Finding Faith When You're Not Even Sure God Is Real* (Grand Rapids, MI: Chosen, 2019), 26–29.

30. Bethany Dawson, "Richard Dawkins' Argument Against Women Having Babies With Down's Syndrome Is Nothing More Than Eugenics," *Independent*, May 18, 2021, https://www.independent.co.uk/voices/richard-dawkins-downs-syndrome-disability-b1848956.html.

31. Alister McGrath, *The Twilight of Atheism: The Rise and Fall of Disbelief in the Modern World* (New York: Doubleday, 2004).

32. Rodney Stark, *The Triumph of Faith: Why the World is More Religious Than Ever* (Wilmington, DE: Intercollegiate Studies Institute, 2015), Kindle.

33. Conservapedia, s.v. "Essay: 2021 Is the WORST Year in the History of Atheism," accessed October 29, 2022, https://www.conservapedia.com/Essay:_2021_is_the_WORST_year_in_the_history_of_atheism.

34. Eric Metaxas, *Is Atheism Dead?* (Washington, DC: Salem Books, 2021).

35. For some reflections on this, see Brown, *Has God Failed You?*; Randy Clark, *The Thrill of Victory—The Agony of Defeat* (Mechanicsburg, PA: Apostolic Network of Global Awakening, 2011). More broadly, and reflecting a different theology of healing, see Randy Alcorn, *If God Is Good: Faith in the Midst of Suffering and Evil* (Sisters, OR: Multnomah, 2009).

36. Poole, "The Four Horsemen Review."

37. Matt Emerson, "C. S. Lewis on Atheist Simplicity," *America: The Jesuit Review*, November 17, 2014, https://www.americamagazine.org/content/ignatian-educator/cs-lewis-atheist-simplicity.

38. Frank Turek, *Stealing From God: Why Atheists Need God to Make Their Case* (Colorado Springs, CO: NavPress, 2015).

39. David Gelernter, "Giving Up Darwin: A Fond Farewell to a Brilliant and Beautiful Theory," *Claremont Review of Books*, Spring 2019, https://claremontreviewofbooks.com/giving-up-darwin/.

40. William A. Dembski, "Defecting From Darwinian Naturalism: A Review of Thomas Nagel's *Mind & Cosmos*," Evolution News & Science Today, November 5, 2012, https://evolutionnews.org/2012/11/defecting_from/.

41. Norman L. Geisler and Frank Turek, *I Don't Have Enough Faith to Be an Atheist* (Wheaton, IL: Crossway, 2004).

42. "Book Review of R. C. Sproul's 'If There's a God, Why Are There Atheists?," Wintery Knight, November 25, 2017, https://winteryknight.com/2017/11/25/book-review-of-r-c-sprouls-if-theres-a-god-why-are-there-atheists-2/.

43. Mary Jordan and *The Washington Post*, "Albania Finds Religion After Decades of Atheism," *Chicago Tribune*, April 18, 2017, https://www.chicagotribune.com/news/ct-xpm-2007-04-18-0704170802-story.html.

44. Oishimaya Sen Nag, "What Religions Are Practiced in Albania?," *World Atlas*, April 10, 2018, https://www.worldatlas.com/articles/what-religions-are-practiced-in-albania.html.

CHAPTER 3

1. See 1 Corinthians 11:1; Philippians 4:9; Hebrews 13:7.

2. Daniel Silliman and Kate Shellnutt, "Ravi Zacharias Hid Hundreds of Pictures of Women, Abuse During Massages, and a Rape Allegation," *Christianity Today*, February 11, 2021, https://www.christianitytoday.com/news/2021/february/ravi-zacharias-rzim-investigation-sexual-abuse-sexting-rape.html.

3. Andrew Prokop, "The Jerry Falwell, Jr. scandal, explained," *Vox*, August 25, 2020, https://www.vox.com/2020/8/25/21399954/jerry-falwell-jr-resigns-scandal-liberty.

4. Lauren Sarner, "Bombshell 'Hillsong' Doc Details Sex Scandals That Battered Celeb Megachurch," *New York Post*, March 23, 2022, https://nypost.com/2022/03/23/bombshell-hillsong-doc-details-carl-lentz-scandal-churchs-cover-ups/.

5. Ruth Graham, "Hillsong, Once a Leader of Christian Cool, Loses Footing in America," *New York Times*, March 29, 2022, updated April 6, 2022, https://www.nytimes.com/2022/03/29/us/hillsong-church-scandals.html.

6. Theresa Waldrop, "Here's What We Know About the Report That Says Southern Baptist Convention Leaders Mishandled Sexual Abuse Allegations," CNN, May 24, 2022, https://www.cnn.com/2022/05/23/us/

southern-baptist-sexual-abuse-report-explainer/index.
html.

7. Sylvie Corbet, "French Report: 330,000 Children
Victims of Church Sex Abuse," AP News, October 5,
2021, https://apnews.com/article/europe-france-child-
abuse-sexual-abuse-by-clergy-religion-ab5da1ff10f905b
1c338a6f3427a1c66.

8. His name is Mike Jones, and he wrote a book titled *I
Had to Say Something: The Art of Ted Haggard's Fall*
(New York, NY: Seven Stories, 2007). The subtitle
makes reference to the name "Art" that Pastor Haggard
used when using Jones' services.

9. Julie R. Thomson, "Can One Bad Apple
Really Spoil a Whole Barrel? We Found Out,"
Huffington Post, July 13, 2016, https://www.
huffpost.com/entry/bad-apples-rotten-good-
ones_n_5784f23ee4b0ed2111d783ff#:~:text=The%20
proverb%20%E2%80%9Cone%20bad%20apple%20
spoils%20the%20barrel%E2%80%9D,causes%20fruit%20
to%20ripen%20%E2%80%95%20is%20to%20blame.

10. See Matthew 19:1–12; 1 Corinthians 7:1–7. Paul also
acknowledged that, unlike him, the other apostles were
married; see 1 Corinthians 9:3–5.

11. Yhomas McKenna, "Cardinal Burke Addresses
the Clergy Scandal," Catholic Action for Faith and
Family, April 2, 2020, https://www.catholicaction.org/
cardinal_burke_addresses_the_clergy_scandal?utm_
campaign=cb_interview_on_scandal&utm_
medium=email&utm_source=catholicaction; see further
https://askdrbrown.org/library/does-catholic-church-
have-homosexual-problem; https://vaticancatholic.com/
seminaries-homosexuality-heresies/.

12. Michael L. Brown, *Has God Failed You? Finding Faith
When You're Not Even Sure God Is Real* (Bloomington,
MN: Chosen Books), 2021.

13. See, for example, Isaiah 19:22; 30:26.

CHAPTER 4

1. Justin McCarthy, "Same-Sex Marriage Support Inches Up to New High of 71%," Gallup, June 1, 2022, https://news.gallup.com/poll/393197/same-sex-marriage-support-inches-new-high.aspx.

2. Matt Walsh (@MattWalshBlog), "It's a good thing that we have a #TransDayofVisibility," Twitter, March 31, 2022, https://twitter.com/MattWalshBlog/status/1509613695621648389.

3. Erin Faith Wilson, "25 Unforgettable Gay TV Kisses," *Advocate*, May 21, 2015, https://www.advocate.com/arts-entertainment/television/2015/05/21/25-unforgettable-gay-tv-kisses?pg=full; and Deborah Hastings, "'L.A. Law' Lesbian Kiss Hailed by Gay Rights Group," AP News, February 8, 1991, https://apnews.com/article/62a4f9c94e3839eddb95916ee43d54f6.

4. Lauren Duca, "Fifteen Years Ago, 'Dawson's Creek' Gave Us TV's First 'Passionate' Gay Kiss. How Far Have We Come?," Huffington Post, April 9, 2015, updated December 6, 2017, https://www.huffpost.com/entry/dawsons-creek-true-love_n_6971230.

5. Mallory Carra, "International Reactions to 'Brokeback Mountain,'" Bustle, December 9, 2015, https://www.bustle.com/articles/127929-brokeback-mountain-was-controversial-10-years-ago-but-how-was-it-received-in-other-countries.

6. Michael L. Brown, "Batman's Robin Is Bi (But Nobody Has an Agenda)," AskDrBrown, August 13, 2021, https://askdrbrown.org/library/batman-s-robin-bi-nobody-has-agenda.

7. Michael L. Brown, "Christian Conservatives You Cannot Put Your Trust in Fox News," Ask Dr. Brown, April 1, 2022, https://askdrbrown.org/library/christian-conservatives-you-cannot-put-your-trust-fox-news.

8. H. Alan Scott, "How Ellen DeGeneres' Coming Out Changed My Life 20 Years Ago," *Newsweek*, April 28, 2017, https://www.newsweek.com/

ellen-degeneres-ellen-degeneres-comes-out-coming-out-ellen-lgbtq-lgbt-gay-gay-591337.

9. See Michael L. Brown, *A Queer Thing Happened to America: And What a Long, Strange Trip It's Been* (Concord, NC: Equal Time Books, 2011), 84–118.

10. Yonat Shimron, "Young Evangelicals Are Leaving Church. LGBTQ Bias May Be Driving Them Away," Religion News Service, August 6, 2021, https://religionnews. com/2021/08/06/young-evangelicals-are-leaving-church-resistance-to-lgbtq-equality-is-driving-them-away/, emphasis added.

11. Jane Timm, "Millennials Leaving Religion Over Anti-Gay Teachings," MSNBC, February 26, 2014, https://www. msnbc.com/morning-joe/millennials-leave-religion-over-gay-issues-msna274871, emphasis added.

12. Paul Bond, "Nearly 40 Percent of U.S. Gen Zs, 30 Percent of Young Christians Identify as LGBTQ, Poll Shows," *Newsweek*, October 20, 2021, https://www.newsweek. com/nearly-40-percent-us-gen-zs-30-percent-christians-identify-lgbtq-poll-shows-1641085.

13. Jeffrey M. Jones, "LGBT Identification in U.S. Ticks Up to 7.1%," Gallup, February 17, 2022, https://news.gallup. com/poll/389792/lgbt-identification-ticks-up.aspx. While Gallup ends Gen Z at 2003, many sources extend the age range to 2012.

14. Eric Kaufmann, "Born This Way? The Rise of LGBT as a Social and Political Identity," Center for the Study of Partisanship and Ideology, May 30, 2022, https:// cspicenter.org/reports/born-this-way-the-rise-of-lgbt-as-a-social-and-political-identity/.

15. Gerald R. Sittser, *Resilient Faith: How the Early Christian "Third Way" Changed the World* (Grand Rapids, MI: Brazos Press, 2019), 11–12; see also Michael Brown, "When the Larger Culture Abandons God and Biblical Values," The Stream, September 16, 2021, https://stream. org/when-the-larger-culture-abandons-god-and-biblical-values/.

16. To watch two relevant debates, see "What Does the Bible Say About Homosexuality? Sean McDowell and Matthew Vines in Conversation," Dr. Sean McDowell, February 3, 2018, YouTube, https://www.youtube.com/watch?v=yFY4VtCWgyI; and "Is Homosexuality Consistent With New Testament Obedience?," Alpha & Omega Ministries, September 19, 2018, YouTube, https://www.youtube.com/watch?v=8oV1bStOK3w&t=2s.

17. "In His Image: Delighting in God's Plan for Gender and Sexuality," In His Image Movie, March 12, 2021, YouTube, https://www.youtube.com/watch?v=W3YKpnrzmqc&t=180s, starting at 2:38.

18. Harriet Sherwood, "'Christianity as Default Is Gone': The Rise of a Non-Christian Europe," *The Guardian*, March 20, 2018, https://www.theguardian.com/world/2018/mar/21/christianity-non-christian-europe-young-people-survey-religion.

19. "LGBT+ Pride 2021 Global Survey Points to a Generation Gap Around Gender Identity and Sexual Attraction," Ipsos, June 9, 2021, https://www.ipsos.com/en/lgbt-pride-2021-global-survey-points-generation-gap-around-gender-identity-and-sexual-attraction.

20. For a sampling of testimonies, see "We Left LGBTQ+ Because We Wanted To," Changed Movement, https://changedmovement.com/.

21. Jonathan Van Maren, "Young People Pushing Back Against Transgender Nonsense Has LGBT Activists Alarmed," LifeSite, July 4, 2019, https://www.lifesitenews.com/blogs/young-people-pushing-back-against-transgender-nonsense-has-lgbt-activists-alarmed/.

22. As summarized by Prof. Jay Richards, Pride month has jumped the shark; see Jay Richards, "Pride Month Jumps the Shark," The Stream, June 13, 2022, https://stream.org/pride-month-jumps-the-shark/.

23. Brooke Migdon, "Support for LGBTQ+ Rights on the Rise: Poll," *The Hill*, March 22, 2022, https://thehill.com/changing-america/respect/equality/599240-support-for-lgbtq-rights-on-the-rise-poll/.

24. Van Maren, "Young People Pushing Back."
25. Van Maren, "Young People Pushing Back."
26. Michael L. Brown, "This Is the Dangerous LGBTQ+ Trajectory That We Have Been Warning About," Ask Dr. Brown, July 6, 2021, https://askdoctorbrown.com/library/dangerous-lgbtq-trajectory-we-have-been-warning-about.
27. See especially Abigail Shrier, *Irreversible Damage: The Transgender Craze Seducing Our Daughters* (Washington, DC: Regnery, 2021).
28. Matt Lamb, "'The Largest Medical Scandal in History': Brave Mom Speaks Out Against Pushing 'Trans' Drugs on Kids," LifeSite, June 20, 2022, https://www.lifesitenews.com/blogs/the-largest-medical-scandal-in-history-brave-mom-speaks-out-against-pushing-trans-drugs-on-kids/?utm_source=top_news&utm_campaign=usa.
29. "r/detrans | Detransition Subreddit," Reddit, accessed September 20, 2022, https://www.reddit.com/r/detrans/wiki/support/.
30. Name withheld, in communication with the author. Used with permission.
31. "A Female-to-Male Transgender Shouts a Warning About Transitioning Children," Ask Dr. Brown, March 2, 2022, YouTube, https://youtu.be/JsNmvH9Alh4.
32. Keira Bell, "Keira Bell: My Story," Persuasion, April 7, 2021, https://www.persuasion.community/p/keira-bell-my-story.
33. Kaufmann, "Born This Way? The Rise of LGBT as a Social and Political Identity."
34. Anjali Singh, "Anxiety and Depression in LGBTQ People," Calm Sage, March 7, 2021, updated June 2, 2022, https://www.calmsage.com/anxiety-and-depression-in-lgbtq-people/.
35. Singh, "Anxiety and Depression."
36. See Michael L. Brown, *The Silencing of the Lambs: The Ominous Rise of Cancel Culture and How We Can Overcome It* (Lake Mary, FL: FrontLine, 2022).

CHAPTER 5

1. Michael L. Brown, "And They Will Know We Are Christians By Our Hate," Ask Dr. Brown, February 17, 2021, https://askdrbrown.org/library/and-they-will-know-we-are-christians-our-hate.

2. Michael L. Brown, *Donald Trump Is Not My Savior: An Evangelical Leader Speaks His Mind About the Man He Supports as President* (Shippensburg, PA: Destiny Image, 2018).

3. Michael L. Brown, *Evangelicals at the Crossroads: Will We Pass the Trump Test?* (Concord, NC: Equal Time Books, 2020).

4. "Transcript: Donald Trump's Taped Comments About Women," *New York Times*, October 8, 2016, https://www.nytimes.com/2016/10/08/us/donald-trump-tape-transcript.html.

5. Andy Stanley, *Not in It to Win It* (Grand Rapids, MI: Zondervan Reflective, 2022), 52–53.

6. See Michael L. Brown, "Recovering the Lost Letter of Jacob," AskDrBrown, March 11, 2013, https://archive.askdrbrown.org/library/recovering-lost-letter-jacob.

7. Stanley, *Not in It to Win It*, 49.

8. Anugrah Kumar, "Hillary Clinton: 'Religious Beliefs... Have to Be Changed' About Abortion," Christian Post, April 25, 2015, https://www.christianpost.com/news/hillary-clinton-religious-beliefs-have-to-be-changed-about-abortion.html.

9. Michael L. Brown, "As Law, Roe Was a Bad Ruling That Always Had to Go," Ask Dr. Brown, June 30, 2022, https://askdrbrown.org/library/law-roe-was-bad-ruling-always-had-go.

10. Daniel Trotta, "Trump Revokes Obama Guidelines on Transgender Bathrooms," Reuters, February 22, 2017, https://www.reuters.com/article/us-usa-trump-lgbt-idUSKBN161243.

11. "Executive Order on Preventing and Combating Discrimination on the Basis of Gender Identity or Sexual Orientation," White House, January 20,

2021, https://www.whitehouse.gov/briefing-room/
presidential-actions/2021/01/20/executive-order-
preventing-and-combating-discrimination-on-basis-of-
gender-identity-or-sexual-orientation/.

12. Thomas Curwen, "CRT, Trumpism and Doubt Roil Biola
University. Is This the Future of Evangelical Christianity?,"
Los Angeles Times, June 10, 2022, updated June 11, 2022,
https://www.latimes.com/california/story/2022-06-10/crt-
trumpism-doubt-roil-biola-university.

CHAPTER 6

1. James A. Stewart, *Evangelism*, 4th ed. (Asheville, NC:
Revival Literature, n.d.), 15.

2. Stewart, *Evangelism*, 15–16, emphasis added.

3. Samuel Chadwick, *The Way to Pentecost* (Fort
Washington, PA: Christian Literature Crusade, 1976),
13.

4. Cited in Michael L. Brown, *From Holy Laughter
to Holy Fire: America on the Edge of Revival*
(Shippensburg, PA: Destiny Image, 1996), 166.

5. See Michael L. Brown, *Hyper-Grace: Exposing the
Dangers of the Modern Grace Message* (Lake Mary, FL:
Charisma House, 2014).

6. Michael L. Brown, "A Compromised Gospel Produces
Compromised Fruit," Ask Dr. Brown, March 12, 2013,
https://askdrbrown.org/library/compromised-gospel-
produces-compromised-fruit.

7. Mark Galli, "The Scandal of the Public Evangelical,"
Christianity Today, July 2, 2009, https://www.
christianitytoday.com/ct/2009/julyweb-only/126-
42.0.html.

8. Brown, "A Compromised Gospel Produces
Compromised Fruit"; "Miss California Carrie
Prejean says racy Web photos posted to mock faith,"
Associated Press, May 5, 2009, https://www.cleveland.
com/people/2009/05/miss_california_carrie_prejean.
html.

9. Brown, "A Compromised Gospel Produces Compromised Fruit"; Carly Wolkoff, "The Game Defends Controversial 'Jesus Piece' Cover," MTV.com, October 30, 2012, https://www.mtv.com/news/3g7w0u/game-jesus-piece-cover; Christine Thomasos, "Rapper 'The Game' Says 'You Can Still Have Swag, Be Christian,'" *The Christian Post*, September 19, 2012, https://www.christianpost.com/news/rapper-the-game-says-you-can-still-have-swag-be-christian.html.

10. My original subject was "Abbreviated Verbal Idioms in the Hebrew Bible: A Comparative Semitic Approach." I don't imagine too many of you are upset that I never finished that.

11. Michael L. Brown, *Playing With Holy Fire: A Wake-Up Call to the Pentecostal-Charismatic Church* (Lake Mary, FL, Charisma House: 2018), 115–116.

12. Brown, *Playing With Holy Fire*, 116–117.

13. Michael L. Brown, *How Saved Are We?* (Shippensburg, PA: Destiny Image, 1990), 16–18.

14. Michael L. Brown, *Revival or We Die: A Great Awakening Is Our Only Hope* (Shippensburg, PA: Destiny Image, 2021), 48–49.

15. For a full-length study, see my book *The Political Seduction of the Church: How Millions of Americans Have Confused Politics With the Gospel* (Washington, DC: Vide Press, 2022).

CHAPTER 7

1. James 1:27; see also 2 Corinthians 6:14–7:1.

2. A. W. Tozer, *This World: Playground or Battleground* (Chicago: The Moody Bible Institute of Chicago, 1989).

3. See, e.g., Ariel Zilber, "Children, Teens Exposed to Online Porn More Likely to Develop Addiction Than Adults," *New York Post*, July 4, 2022, https://nypost.com/2022/07/04/children-teens-exposed-to-online-porn-more-likely-to-develop-addiction-than-adults/.

4. Michael L. Brown and Nancy Brown, *Breaking the Stronghold of Food: How We Conquered Food*

Addictions and Discovered a New Way of Living (Lake Mary, FL: Siloam, 2017), 55.

5. Serah Louis, "'We've Seen People Go From Six-Figure Incomes...to Living on the Streets': Why It's Easier Than Ever to Get Addicted to Gambling," MoneyWise, July 11, 2022, https://moneywise.com/managing-money/debt/gambling-addictions-on-rise-robbing-americans-of-livelihoods.

6. Louis, "'We've Seen People Go From Six-Figure Incomes.'"

7. Will Yakowicz, "U.S. Gambling Revenue Hit Record $53 Billion In 2021," *Forbes*, February 15, 2022, https://www.forbes.com/sites/willyakowicz/2022/02/15/us-gambling-revenue-hit-record-53-billion-in-2021/.

8. Blue Letter Bible, s.v. "anomia," accessed September 20, 2022, https://www.blueletterbible.org/lexicon/g458/kjv/tr/0-1/.

9. See Matthew 5:27–30; 18:6–9; Mark 9:42–48.

10. Name withheld, in communication with the author. Used with permission.

11. Some of the preceding paragraphs were adapted from Michael L. Brown, *Go and Sin No More: A Call to Holiness* (Concord, NC: Equal Time Books, 1999); for *acharit* in Proverbs, see 5:4, 5:11; 14:12; 14:13; 16:25; 19:20; 20:21; 23:18, 23:32; 24:14, 24:20; 25:8; 29:21; Blue Letter Bible, s.v. "*aḥărît*," accessed October 17, 2022, https://www.blueletterbible.org/lexicon/h319/kjv/wlc/0-1/.

CHAPTER 8

1. Frank Newport, "Fewer in U.S. Now See Bible as Literal Word of God," Gallup, July 6, 2022, https://news.gallup.com/poll/394262/fewer-bible-literal-word-god.aspx.

2. "The Holy Torah—the First Five Books of Moses," Hebrew for Christians, accessed October 31, 2022, https://hebrew4christians.com/Scripture/Torah/torah.html.

3. "Marduk Creates the World From the Spoils of Battle," Bruce Railsback's Geoscience Resources, accessed October 31, 2022, www.railsback.org/CS/CSMarduk.html.

4. E. A. Speiser, in J. B. Pritchard, ed., *The Ancient Near Eastern Texts Relating to the Old Testament* (3rd ed. with Supplement; Princeton, NJ: Princeton University Press, 1969), 63.

5. Brown, *Saving a Sick America*, 61–62.

6. The Bible speaks of the Jewish people being scattered around the world, yet preserved through great suffering, then being brought back to the land of Israel with Jerusalem as the capital city, against which the nations of the earth will align themselves at the end of the age.

7. See Brown, *Has God Failed You?* and Michael L. Brown, *Compassionate Father or Consuming Fire: Engaging the God of the Old Testament* (Jacksonville, FL: AWKNG Press, 2021).

CHAPTER 9

1. Since it is the Bible which tells us about the flood, we should understand the Bible's explanation for the flood. According to Genesis 6, the human race was destroying itself through violence and perversion, and if left to ourselves, we would have made an end of our race. To spare us, ultimately making the way for you and me to be born and have the possibility of being in God's family forever, He found one righteous man on the planet, named Noah (just think of what that says about everyone else!) and through Noah's sons and daughters-in-law, gave humanity a second chance. The flood, then, although devastating and severe, was also an act of mercy.

2. Some might point to Deuteronomy 28:63, speaking of God bringing curses of judgment on His disobedient people: "And as the LORD once delighted in making you prosperous and many, so will the LORD now delight in causing you to perish and in wiping you out; you shall be torn from the land that you are about to

enter and possess" (JPS TANAKH). Doesn't this point to God enjoying these acts of devastating judgment? The answer is that this one verse must be balanced against scores of others verses where the Lord expresses His desire that His people will do what is right so that He can bless them and where He states that He too suffers when His people suffer. As He said through Jeremiah, "I will surely gather them from all the lands where I banish them in my furious anger and great wrath; I will bring them back to this place and let them live in safety. They will be my people, and I will be their God. I will give them singleness of heart and action, so that they will always fear me and that all will then go well for them and for their children after them. I will make an everlasting covenant with them: I will never stop doing good to them, and I will inspire them to fear me, so that they will never turn away from me. I will rejoice in doing them good and will assuredly plant them in this land with all my heart and soul" (Jer. 32:37–41). We should see the verse in Deuteronomy, as an example of hyperbolic speech to drive home a point, also recognizing that whatever God does is perfect and just, and therefore, even when He brings deserved punishment, it is for a good purpose, and He feels no internal contradiction when inflicting judgment.

3. The Hebrew literally speaks of "thousands," which many translators understand to mean people, rather than "a thousand," which is then interpreted to mean "generations." Yet the contrast with "third and fourth" suggests that "a thousand generations" (or, even more literally, "thousands of generations") is the best way to understand the text. Either way, the contrast between mercy and judgment is meant to be dramatic.

4. Jennifer Rosenberg, "The Major Wars and Conflicts of the 20th Century," ThoughtCo., updated January 28, 2020, https://www.thoughtco.com/major-wars-and-conflicts-20th-century-1779967.

5. Wikipedia, s.v. "*The Black Book of Communism,*"
    updated October 29, 2022, https://en.wikipedia.org/wiki/
    The_Black_Book_of_Communism#Memorial_analysis.

6. "How Many Nuclear Weapons Does the US Have?,"
    USAFacts, April 12, 2022, updated May 5, 2022, https://
    usafacts.org/articles/how-many-nuclear-weapons-does-
    the-us-have/.

7. "What Is the Most Powerful Weapon in the US
    Arsenal?," Lemielleux, March 10, 2022, https://
    lemielleux.com/what-is-the-most-powerful-weapon-in-
    the-us-arsenal/.

8. See the chapter "Permission to Doubt" in Brown, *Has
    God Failed You?*

9. C. S. Lewis, *The Problem of Pain, in The Complete
    C. S. Lewis Signature Classics* (San Francisco:
    HarperSanFrancisco, 2007), 620–621.

10. Stephen Eyre, "C. S. Lewis on Heaven and Hell," C. S.
    Lewis Institute, September 8, 2018, https://www.
    cslewisinstitute.org/resources/c-s-lewis-on-heaven-and-
    hell/.

11. Eyre, "C. S. Lewis on Heaven and Hell."

12. While we can debate the nature of future punishment,
    based on the whole testimony of the Bible, I am
    convinced that we must reject universalism, the concept
    that everyone will eventually be saved.

CHAPTER 10

1. See again the chapter "Permission to Doubt" in Brown,
    Has God Failed You?

2. Craig S. Keener, *Miracles: The Credibility of the
    New Testament Accounts* (Grand Rapids, MI: Baker
    Academic, 2011).

3. For a popular, condensed version, see Craig S. Keener,
    *Miracles Today: The Supernatural Work of God in the
    Modern World* (Grand Rapids, MI: Baker Academic,
    2021).

4. See Vishal Mangalwadi, *The Book That Made Your
    World: How the Bible Created the Soul of Western*

Civilization (Nashville, TN: Thomas Nelson, 2012).
More broadly, see Alvin J. Schmidt, *How Christianity Changed the World* (Grand Rapids, MI: Zondervan, 2004); Dinesh D'Souza, What's So Great About Christianity? (Washington, DC: Regnery, 2007). For an honest assessment of the good and bad in Christian history, see John Dickson, *Bullies and Saints: An Honest Look at the Good and Evil of Christian History* (Grand Rapids, MI: Zondervan Reflective, 2021).

5. Robyn Roste, "Skillet's John Cooper Is Deconstructing Deconstruction," Faith Strong Today, January 28, 2021, https://faithstrongtoday.com/robynroste/skillets-john-cooper-is-deconstructing-deconstruction.

CHAPTER 11

1. Quotable Quote (Stephen Roberts), Goodreads, accessed October 31, 2022, https://www.goodreads.com/quotes/17095-i-contend-that-we-are-both-atheists-i-just-believe.
2. Peter Kupisz, "Atheists Simply Believe in 'One Less God'?" Worldview Summit, accessed October 31, 2022, https://www.worldviewsummit.org/post/atheists-simply-believe-in-one-less-god.
3. Nicholas Rizzo, "32 Bible Sales Statistics [2022]," WordsRated, February 2, 2022, https://wordsrated.com/bible-sales-statistics/.
4. Hemant Mehta endorsement of Dan Barker's *God: The Most Unpleasant Character in All Fiction* (New York: Union Square & Co., 2016), back cover.
5. "Most Popular Bible Verse and Top Search Terms Tell a Story of Faith in 2020," YouVersion, December 2, 2020, https://www.youversion.com/press/youversion-names-verse-of-the-year-and-releases-2020s-bible-app-search-trends.
6. "Bibles: Dangerous, Illegal, Covert," Love Packages, April 20, 2019, https://lovepackages.org/bibles-dangerous-illegal-covert/.

7. Randall Murphree, "'The Jesus Film' Celebrates 25 Years, Billions of Viewers," Crosswalk, May 6, 2004, https://www.crosswalk.com/culture/features/the-jesus-film-celebrates-25-years-billions-of-viewers-1260850.html#:~:text=The%20movie%27s%20cumulative%20viewing%20and%20listening%20audience%20%28multiple,languages%2C%20making%20it%20the%20world%27s%20most%20translated%20film.

8. Michael L. Brown, *Job: The Faith to Challenge God: A New Translation and Commentary* (Peabody, MA: Hendrickson Publishers, 2019); Brown, *Has God Failed You?*, 143–157.

9. "The Christian Ideal," Society of G. K. Chesterton, April 29, 2012, https://www.chesterton.org/the-christian-ideal/.

10. John G. Lake, *Spiritual Hunger and Other Sermons*, ed. Gordon Lindsay (Dallas, TX: Christ for the Nations, 1987), 7.

11. In this passage, Paul is quoting from Isaiah 40:13 and Job 41:11.

ABOUT THE AUTHOR

S INCE COMING TO faith in 1971 as a sixteen-year-old, heroin-shooting, hippie rock drummer, Michael Brown has devoted his life to awakening the church, sparking moral and cultural revolution in society, and reaching out to his own Jewish people. He has preached throughout America and around the world, bringing a message of repentance, revival, and reformation. He has a PhD in Near Eastern Languages and Literatures from New York University and has served as a visiting or adjunct professor at Southern Evangelical Seminary, Gordon Conwell Theological Seminary (Charlotte), Trinity *Evangelical* Divinity School, Fuller Theological Seminary, Denver Theological Seminary, King's Seminary, Regent University School of Divinity, and Global Awakening Theological Seminary. He is also the host of the nationally syndicated *Line of Fire* radio broadcast and the founder and president of FIRE School of Ministry.

The author of more than forty books, including *The Silencing of the Lambs*, the five-volume series *Answering Jewish Objections to Jesus*, and commentaries on Jeremiah and Job, Dr. Brown has contributed numerous articles to scholarly publications, most notably the *Oxford Dictionary of Jewish Religion* and the *Theological Dictionary of the Old Testament*. He has also written more than twenty-five hundred op-ed pieces that have appeared in the Daily Wire, *Newsweek*, *Townhall*, Christian Post, The Stream, the *Jerusalem Post*,

Haaretz, World Net Daily, *Charisma News,* One News Now, Times of Israel, and other sites.

Dr. Brown has debated Jewish rabbis, agnostic professors, and gay activists on radio, TV, and college campuses, and he is widely considered to be the world's foremost Messianic Jewish apologist. He and his wife, Nancy, who is also a Jewish believer, have been married since 1976. They have two daughters and four grandchildren.

For access to hundreds of hours of free content, visit AskDrBrown.org and sign up for Dr. Brown's informational emails. You can also download the AskDrBrown Ministries app on the Apple and Android platforms.